"This book has some very good ideas on how couples can stop their anger at each other and live more successfully together."

> —Albert Ellis, Ph.D., noted psychologist and author of *A Guide to Rational Living*

"Bull's-eye! Like a Zen archer, Barton Goldsmith releases an arrow into the very center of intimacy. And like a Zen monk he writes with a disarming charm and graceful elegance, creating a book that is fun, funny, yet penetratingly wise. My advice is simple—Read it."

> —Shawn Christopher Shea, MD, author of *Happiness Is* and *Psychiatric Interviewing: the Art of Understanding*

"Goldsmith is the BEST natural born therapist I have ever met. I thoroughly enjoy working with him."

> —David Viscott, MD, TV and radio talk show host and author of *The Making of a Psychiatrist*

"I can HONESTLY say that Goldsmiths's book is outstanding—a really terrific combination of good bedside manner, useful and practical information, and common sense."

> —Anne Sheffield, award winning author of *Depression Fallout* and *How You Can Survive When They're Depressed*

"At last a book that not only guides the reader when it comes to successful relationships but shows us the value of emotional fitness: communication, nurturance and constancy, in partnering. By subscribing to Goldsmith's theory and practice, couples will end up with a more satisfying connection and a better sense of each other's needs, as well as their own."

> —Susan Shapiro Barash, author of
> *The New Wife: The Evolving Role
> of the American Wife*

"Love is all you need—but, you also need a well-written, easy-to-follow roadmap to the heartland. Renown relationship guru Barton Goldsmith has provided this map in *Emotional Fitness*. It is your guidebook to revitalizing your relationship."

> —Jeffrey K. Zeig, Ph.D., director of
> the Milton Erickson Foundation and
> organizer of the Evolution of
> Psychotherapy Conference

"In *Emotional Fitness for Couples*, Goldsmith helps couples become proactive in their relationships by using easy to follow exercises and practical advice that allows them to enhance their interactions and their love."

> —Gerald G. Jampolsky, MD, author of
> *Love Is Letting Go of Fear*

Emotional Fitness

for Couples

10 Minutes
a Day to a
Better
Relationship

BARTON GOLDSMITH, PH.D.

New Harbinger Publications, Inc.

Publisher's Note

Distributed in Canada by Raincoast Books

Copyright © 2005 by Barton Goldsmith
New Harbinger Publications, Inc.
5674 Shattuck Avenue
Oakland, CA 94609
www.newharbinger.com

Cover and text design by Amy Shoup; Acquired by Melissa Kirk

Author photo courtesy of The Ventura County Star, Ventura, CA

All Rights Reserved. Printed in the United States of America.

Library of Congress Cataloging-in-Publication Data

Goldsmith, Barton.
  Emotional fitness for couples : 10 minutes a day to a better relationship/ Barton Goldsmith.
    p. cm.
  Includes bibliographical references.
  ISBN-10 1-57224-439-9
  ISBN-13 978-1-57224-439-9
  1. Couples. 2. Intimacy. 3. Love. 4. Communication in marriage. 5. Man-woman relationships. I. Title.
  HQ801.G5875 2006
  646.7'8—dc22
2005029512

18 17

25 24 23 22 21 20 19 18

Table of Contents

Acknowledgments

$\mathcal{I}$ am a team, and am deeply indebted to a cadre of friends, colleagues, and mentors. I am grateful for your support, guidance, cheerleading, and contributions to my life and work. Without you all, I know that this work could not have been accomplished.

Thanks to Tim Gallagher, publisher of *The Ventura County Star*, for liking my articles enough to give them a chance, and to Scripps-Howard News Service for nationally syndicating them. Thank you also to my readers, who prodded me to write this book.

At KCLU Radio, Mary Olson, Jim Rondeau, Mia Kranatz-Shifflett, Teresa Olson, and the staff and listeners make me feel like a member of the family and do an amazing job producing *Emotional Fitness* for radio. Special thanks to my cohost, Pamela Michaels, and my right hands, Wendy Simpson Cherry, Chris Springhorn, and Mary Beth Trudeau, who are always here for me.

To my friends, teachers, and colleagues Dr. William Glasser; Linda Metzger, MFT; Scott James, Ph.D.; Albert

Ellis, Ph.D.; Stephen Trudeau, Psy.D.; Harville Hendrix, Ph.D.; Louise L. Hay; Dr. Ned Hallowell; and Dr. Bernie Siegel; many thanks.

To my mentors Dr. Elisabeth Kubler-Ross, who directed me to this new life, bless you; and to Dr. David Viscott, who gave me the highest compliment I have ever received and allowed me to learn from him, thank you.

Thanks also to my friends Jan Gilmore, Laurie Butler, Trygve Duryea, and Michael Park, who always listened. As well as to my writing mentors and editors Melissa Kirk, Brady Kahn, Ed Rigsbee, Geri Knilans, Kim Lamb-Gregory, and Karen Allen.

To my almost-a-daughter Keaton Talmadge, and Christine, Rafi and Anna Khardalian, and Piewacket, my narcissistic black cat, all of whom taught me that life is a gift and not every person who crosses my path is worth rubbing up against.

And most of all, I thank my clients, who have given me the greatest gift of all: their trust.

This book is dedicated to Silva,
who, with her open heart, continues to teach me, tease me,
inspire me, and make me a better man.

What Is Emotional Fitness?

$\mathcal{I}$n my state of California (sometimes called the State of Confusion), health and fitness are highly valued, and people focus a lot of time and energy on their appearance and on getting their bodies fit. Many people change their lifestyles, go on all kinds of bizarre regimens and diets, and take numerous supplements and even medications in order to lose weight.

In comparison, very little energy is put toward getting and keeping our emotional selves and our primary relationships in shape. Sadly, many people put more time and energy into their hair than into their relationships (this is where Dr. Phil and I have an advantage over many men) and then complain about the lack of intimacy and satisfaction in their personal lives. The reason why some relationships work and many others don't is that couples in those working relationships *work* on them.

The most difficult part about achieving emotional fitness in a relationship can be figuring out exactly what to do or what to talk about in order to get there. It's hard for us to look inside and discover which parts of our emotional selves need to be in better shape. That is why I have written this book.

Getting your relationship emotionally fit requires doing something about it on a regular basis. With physical exercise, the more we do, the easier it gets, and emotional fitness works the same way. Unlike a physical workout, however, getting and staying emotionally fit can take as little as ten minutes a day and involve only small changes here and there. When you consider the value of the results, this is an extraordinarily good investment.

So put down the remote control, let the weeds in your garden grow a little longer, and send the kids to a movie, so the two of you can be alone and chat about your lives together.

How to Use This Book

This book explains in a straightforward manner how you can achieve a closer relationship with your partner, overcome difficulties, and develop not only deeper communication but a deeper emotional connection—all of which leads to the ability to have more fun together and a healthy sex life. Here is how I recommend getting the most out of the process. Start by finding a chapter that deals with one of the issues that is present in your relationship. If the chapter is helpful, share it with your partner. Next, talk about it and commit to making one of the suggested changes, and then do one of the exercises.

You can then read the book from the beginning or pick another chapter that really speaks to the issues that are in your face at the moment. The most important part is that you quickly share any insights or realizations with your partner.

I designed this book to be fifty-two chapters so that if you read just one a week, it will help you to keep your relationship on the positive track. The idea was to make it as simple and as easy as possible. Reading and talking about each chapter can take as little as ten minutes. You can take longer if you wish, but don't spend hours on one issue. Spending too much time on one thing can wear a relationship down. Start slowly for now (ten minutes a day), and, if you're so moved, work yourself up to an hour once a week. That's all most couples need.

After you've experienced a little success with some communication or emotional exercise, making it a practice in your relationship will be less intimidating. A number of couples I know actually take the time to talk about their relationships during evening walks or while bike riding. This casual approach can work well because you release your emotional anxiety through physical exercise.

So congratulate yourself and your partner. You are about to move your relationship forward and create a safer and more loving space in your life. Trust your own process, and if you get lost or confused remember that you will always be able to find your way through your life's issues by looking within yourself. All it takes is patience, persistence, and ten minutes a day.

PART 1

Love

The Weekly Relationship Meeting

One of the things that going to therapy as a couple provides is an accountability factor. This comes from knowing you are working on your relationship. If you are in counseling, your therapist holds both of you accountable to do the work.

All couples need to have a method for helping each other stay focused or accountable to their relationships. One of the things I believe in strongly is having a weekly relationship meeting. This is where you discuss your feelings openly, so you keep resentments from taking root.

The goals of the weekly relationship meeting are for you to increase awareness, develop deeper communication, bring greater peace and harmony into your lives. The support and understanding that can come from these meetings will make your relationship richer and deeper.

♡ *Here are some simple guidelines to help you get started. Remember that all relationships are different and not every step may be exactly right for yours, so be creative and adjust the guidelines when necessary.*

1. *Connect with your partner. Do this by holding hands and looking into each other's eyes. Verbally thank each other for participating in this process. This lets your partner know you are present emotionally as well as physically. Ask each other how you are feeling right now.*

2. *Keep it upbeat. Begin by acknowledging what the two of you have done well over the past week. You can start the discussion by talking about the nicest things that happened. Encourage each other to talk about feelings, not just tasks. This will make it much easier to make changes.*

3. *Make the commitment to do this every week. Consistency is the key to making this process and your relationship work. In a short time, you will enjoy the focused attention and look forward to this time together.*

4. *Remember the basic rules of communication. There is a speaker and a listener, the speaker speaks while the listener listens without getting defensive or accusatory. Start by each of you taking three minutes to say what's on your mind.*

5. *Talk about things that matter. Don't hold on to feelings that are making you uncomfortable. This is the time to present your issues in a calm and constructive way. In areas where there have been difficulties, point them out gently and don't be punitive.*

6. *Help each other heal old issues. Is there anything that is still unresolved? Did you both keep your commitments? Make sure you follow up on past decisions so that you keep the trust in each other and the process. Once you agree that an issue is resolved, there is no need to rehash it.*

7. *Discuss future plans. Talk about the calendar for the coming week and the future, both near and far. Happiness comes from moving toward what you want, so make sure you always have goals and dreams.*

8. *Fun of some kind should follow each meeting. Some couples make this their weekly date night, and others cook together or get takeout and a DVD. Whatever works for both of you is fine, as long as you're having some fun.*

9. *Work toward compromise and consensus. Win-lose is the same as lose-lose. Avoid this situation by talking until you both agree or at least agree to disagree. Remember that the purpose here is to bring you closer together. Encourage one another to participate fully in the meeting.*

10. *When the discussion ends, consolidate the gains you have made and share the vision and the goals of your relationship. It may be helpful to write down your decisions. Be sure to acknowledge each other for participating in this process.*

Love Is a Verb

In school, they taught us that a verb was an action word, and "love" is a verb. It is not something you get by waiting for it, and it is not something you give by just thinking about it. People who have difficulty expressing loving feelings may say that their partner "knows they love them," so they don't need to tell them. They may go on to explain that just because they don't say "I love you" doesn't mean they don't have loving feelings. Their partners usually respond by saying something like, "Yes, I know you love me, but I need to hear it once in a while. It gives me strength."

Everyone needs emotional support at times, and a simple "I love you" can give someone the security they need to feel comfortable in a relationship. Not knowing you are loved breeds insecurity and discontent, and no one can be completely sure of what another person is thinking or feeling. Giving emotional support to your partner will make them feel more secure and will encourage them to give more to the relationship. It creates a safe space for the two of you to grow together and deal with the difficulties of life that are sure to arise.

Some misguided people believe that keeping their partner off balance or unsure is a way to maintain control in the relationship. This type of manipulation can cause long-term relationship problems. A relationship is not a game, it is a gift. Withholding love and support from your partner will only cause harm.

If speaking the words "I love you" is a difficult task, there are many other ways that you can say "I love you" without actually verbalizing it. Some people use codes to express feelings that they have difficulty saying directly. A great example of how this works can be seen in the movie *Ghost*. The character played by Demi Moore would tell Patrick Swayze's character that she loved him and he always responded by saying, "Ditto." This coded "I love you" was something only the two of them shared and it played an important role in the plot.

If saying "I love you" is difficult for you, you can use other words or take other actions that mean the same thing. If words fail you altogether, then a certain look, a touch, even a small gift, like a single flower, can be enough to communicate your feelings. Many things can work. A British woman who attended one of my workshops shared,

"I know my husband is saying 'I love you' when he pats me on my bottom." This was their code.

I also know two happily married, busy professionals who always page each other with "111," meaning, "I love you." The other reciprocates with "111-2," or, "I love you, too." These two manage to strengthen their relationship, even with their busy schedules, by letting each other know they're thinking of the other person throughout the day.

♡ *Create your own personal "I love you" code to show your partner that you care. Keep it your little secret, something that only the two of you share. It's easy to develop a code. The next time your partner says, "I love you," first respond in kind (say, "I love you") then add your own extra touch.*

Soon, that extra touch will have a life of its own and may well become an important part of your lives. It could mean as much, if not more, than saying those sometimes difficult words "I love you." Try this for a week and at the end of the week (during a romantic dinner), ask your partner how they feel about it.

Let the Good Times Roll

$\mathcal{T}$he course of working through a healing process in your relationship can be a burden. You can spend so much time working things out that you forget the reason you came together in the first place. Sometimes you stop doing those things that created the fond memories you are trying to hold on to.

Sometimes it's important to put aside the working-it-out process and just have a good time. This gives you a chance to allow the other feelings you are processing to settle and find their proper place. It gives you an opportunity to reconnect on a different, yet familiar level.

We can forget how to play with each other because our competitive lifestyles have taught us how to play against each other. Playing with your partner will help heal your relationship. Remembering how to have fun takes a little time and experimentation, but, like riding a bike, it's something you never forget.

Having fun doesn't require a great deal of time or expense. In fact, as a couple it can be really enjoyable doing mundane things around the house. Even cleaning out a closet can prove to be more of a treasure hunt than a chore as you talk about the memories brought up by the things you find.

Doing things like this with your partner can turn a simple task into a creative exercise, and you will discover some new qualities about each other.

Other fun and inexpensive activities like going to swap meets, taking walks, and cooking together can be very intimate. You also can play games, dance in the living room, or just go for a drive. Creating a break in your normal routine can be as easy as doing nice things for no good reason.

Romance should also be fun. Most couples don't plan time to be together romantically, and so it happens less and less frequently. A good romantic relationship can create a lot of fulfillment, and little things can be very romantic. Have you ever brought home a single rose for your partner or sent them a card? Do you kiss often and when least expected?

Playing with your partner is as important as being there in a crisis. It says that you care, and it gives you both a break from dealing with the day-to-day issues we all face.

So kiss each other, hold hands, and create some fun in your world.

♡ *The idea here is to add some fun and romance into your lives by thinking and acting outside the box. Try taking a bubble bath by candlelight together. Put aside any pre-conceptions, and don't worry about spilling water on the floor. Just plan to be together in a fun way. Do something outside the box at least once a week.*

Sometimes Being There Is Enough

*W*hen your partner is talking to you, do you ever feel like you're not really there? When a loved one is in emotional pain, have you tried to give comfort and advice, but it didn't feel like you could say the right thing?

We have all experienced this dilemma, which occurs when our minds and hearts are somewhere else. This is something that is easy to change if you know how.

Most of the time, other people just need to know we are present before they can open up. Unfortunately, we seldom take the time to make the connections needed to let our loved ones know we are really there for them.

Too many times, daily hassles or unexpected events can distract us and make us seem unavailable. When that is the case, and your loved one wants to talk, you may be listening with your ears but not feeling with your hearts. You have to learn to listen with your "third ear," which means to listen for the feeling behind what is being said.

Your partner may just need someone to listen. There are also many times when just holding your loved one and letting them cry on your shoulder is all that is needed; words may not be necessary.

You can also acknowledge the feelings being expressed. Saying something like "I understand that it made you sad" will validate your loved one and help them move through their issues. This process is called *active listening*.

Sometimes you might suspect there is something on your partner's mind that they are unable to share with you. You may sense your loved one is in pain but is unable to speak to you about how they are feeling. Asking directly, "Is something bothering you?" can be the key to opening the right door. Once the feelings are expressed, everyone feels better.

If your partner can't verbalize their feelings at the moment, be patient and don't take it personally. They are dealing with their own emotions, not yours. It is important to give them the space to share their feelings when they are ready to do so. Just let them know you are there for them, and when the time is right, they will express themselves.

Take the example of Barney and Betty. They have been together for twenty years and have had a good relationship and life. Recently, Barney had become less communicative with Betty. She did the right thing and asked him what was wrong. She also told him that when he was ready to talk, she was there for him. For several days, Betty gently reminded Barney that she was his partner for life and wanted to share everything with him, even his problems.

One night after dinner as they sat on the sofa and held hands, Barney finally opened up to Betty. With tears in his eyes, he told her he had to have some medical tests that were very frightening. He confided to her that if something serious was going on, he did not want to burden her with it.

Betty held him while he released his feelings and tears. They went through the tests together. Betty was always there, holding his hand. The process lasted several weeks, and everything turned out fine (other than Barney having to give up beer nuts). Going through this experience together made them a closer couple and added depth to their relationship.

It doesn't take a lot of encouragement for people who are full of emotions to express their feelings if they know they have a safe place. A sincere look or an honest hug can break down many walls. Remember that it doesn't always take words, but in all ways, it takes heart.

♡ *Learning to make a deeper connection is not as hard as it sounds. Do this simple exercise with your partner, and try to have fun with it.*

Take your partner's hands, look into one another's eyes, and then remember what it is that you love about your partner. Do this for just a couple of minutes and you will actually begin to feel a deeper link with one another.

Done on a regular basis (nightly or even once a week), this exercise will bring you closer together by helping the two of you connect at a heart level. I recommend that you do this before having a deep conversation.

Give Without Expectation

All that we give to others comes back to us—the good and the bad. Giving of ourselves allows us to feel the fullness life has to offer. One of the reasons we fall in love is because we want to give the best part of ourselves. The purpose of life is to share our gifts with the world. This is one of life's secrets, and it will provide you with a great deal of happiness if you allow it to.

Sometimes we give with the idea of getting something back. This takes place in our relationships more times than we may realize. It's important to learn to give in ways that respect the people you love, to give without expectations and heal misunderstanding with communication, not presents.

Some people have the need to give too much. If you feel this is something you do, take some time to look at your behavior more closely. Are you giving because you feel unworthy? This type of generosity is actually a compulsive behavior, and you may be giving more than what you can afford—materially and emotionally.

There are also times in relationships when we misunderstand the true needs of those we love. When our own guilt or the desire to placate someone is behind the giving, it's really a form of manipulation. This can only cause resentment because the real issues never get resolved.

On the other hand, giving because someone else demands it is also a sign that something in the relationship is not healthy. Giving is a choice. You give because you want to, not because you have to. If giving becomes uncomfortable, you need to take a step away and look at your motivation.

Similarly, trying to buy affection never works because people who accept such gifts will never get enough. The giver is always left with the feeling of not doing anything right, and their lowered self-esteem makes the giver less attractive.

If you are caught in this trap, you may want to reevaluate your relationship. People who truly care about you will prefer to receive acts of love rather than gifts. For a truly loving person, gifts from the heart, like breakfast in bed or a love note, mean more than diamonds or gold.

Learning to give in a healthy manner requires understanding how you each can get your needs met. Both the giver and receiver must be honored in the giving cycle, and true giving always comes from the heart. As you learn how to give and receive, you'll find the right balance.

♡ *Try making a list of favorite nonmaterial things you'd love to get from your partner (back rubs, candlelight dinners, foot massages, breakfast in bed, and so on). Then exchange lists with your partner and make it a goal to do something from each other's list every week.*

Ten Tips to Improve Your Relationship

I have often been asked, "What makes a relationship work?" The following list covers some of the things couples in successful relationships do.

Pick one and see how it works for you, and then try another. Not everything is going to work for everybody, but using any one of these tips will improve your relationship.

1. *Have a relationship meeting where you talk face to face once a week.*

   This should be a private, uninterrupted time during which you and your partner focus only on each other. Here are some ideas to include in your session: connect with each other by holding hands and looking into each other's eyes; decide if you are going to talk about what's going on right now or resolve old issues; share the vision and goals of your relationship; end the evening with a "date" or fun activity after the discussion. See chapter 1 for a detailed outline.

2. *Make sure you have your partner's attention before you talk about an important issue.*

   To communicate, you first must agree to listen and make sure you are being heard. Simply ask, "Is this a good time for us to talk?" Never try to hold a conversation when your partner's attention is focused on something else. If it's not a good time, don't try to force the conversation. Instead, schedule a time when you both will be able to give each other your full attention. During crises, however, remember that your partner needs you now, not later. At these times be sensitive, drop what you are doing, and be prepared to listen and talk.

3. *Give in on the little things.*

Save your energy for what's most important, and be willing to give in on the small stuff. Few things will do more to improve your relationship, and when you give in on the little stuff, bigger things tend to go your way. If you are both invested in an issue, assign a rating (on a scale of 1 to 10) to see who should give in. When something is a 10 for your partner but only a 5 for you, give in. This also works well with family and children.

4. *Find ways to say "I love you" without saying the words "I love you."*

Practice random acts of kindness with your partner. Leave coded messages. Do nice things for no reason. In other words, do all the little things you did when courting your lover that have now fallen by the wayside. Give to your partner in the ways he or she wishes to be given to. See chapter 2 for more ideas on how to show you care.

5. *If you are hurt or angry, communicate your feelings in a loving, constructive way as soon as circumstances permit.*

One of the quickest ways to kill a relationship is to nurse grudges and harbor resentment. These never lead to positive outcomes; they only lead to unkindness, anger and sadness. If you are uncomfortable talking to your partner about issues, find someone else to talk to. You must find an outlet for your frustrations, or they will creep in and damage your relationship. See chapter 30.

6. *Be a team player.*

You can't be in a relationship for yourself; both parties have to give 100 percent to get 100 percent. One good tool for working on your relationship is to create a "wish list" of fun things you would like to do with your partner. List three or four things you would like to do in the next few weeks. These should be simple, fun things that are easy to do, and each spouse should be willing to go along with the other's list. In effect, you and your partner are granting each other a wish, so don't put something on the list that will cause major conflict. See chapter 3 for more ideas on how to have fun together.

7. Work on your relationship.

The biggest difference between relationships that work and those that don't is that the couples in the relationships that work *work on them*. This keeps you from taking each other for granted. You have to be committed to making a relationship work, and part of that commitment means doing the necessary work.

8. Create new goals together.

You need to reevaluate your goals once you have achieved some or all of them because happiness comes from moving toward what you want, not getting it. Creating new goals together can help create deeper understanding and strengthen a loving relationship.

9. Fight fair.

Conflict in relationships is inevitable. If you fight fair, a conflict can be resolved in a positive, constructive manner. See chapter 40 for more information on how to do this.

10. *Act romantic and you will feel romantic.*

When it comes to sex, don't wait for the "mood" to come over you. Set the scene, play the part, and you will be surprised how easily the romantic feelings come. See chapter 23 for more ideas.

PART
2

Intimacy

Why Do We
Run from Intimacy?

Getting close is hard, and remaining close is harder. Many people have a fear of intimacy, which may compel them to sabotage a relationship when it reaches a certain level of depth or closeness.

Fear of intimacy can manifest itself in different forms, such as feeling that the relationship is not good enough. Some people fear getting lost in the overpowering sense of closeness; they actually fear the relationship getting too good. One moment they can feel the wonderful rapture of intimacy and in the next moment be terrified they will lose themselves. This fear drives them to say or do things unconsciously that prevent intimacy. This fear can be overwhelming and repel them away from intimate relationships and sometimes toward people who may not be emotionally available. They may be attracted to people who are unstable in their own lives or just totally unsuited to them. For some, this makes having a relationship safe because, on an unconscious level, the couple knows it won't work out.

When people who fear intimacy do find someone who might actually make a good partner, they find some way to hurt them or push them away. They may think that they are asserting their own independence or that they don't need anyone else in their lives. Running away from intimacy does not set us free. It controls us.

If you have fears of intimacy, it is possible to get over them and allow yourself to be close to someone. First, you have to become aware that you have this issue. You also have to learn to believe that intimacy will not dissolve you into nothingness, smother you, or ruin your productivity. The truth is that intimacy will enhance your finer qualities and reduce your negative ones. You do not lose your power when you truly love someone; you increase it.

It is not uncommon for some people to mistake codependency or desperation for intimacy. Not being able to tell where one of you begins and the other ends is not intimacy; it is enmeshment. But needing someone for the right reasons is not a sign of weakness; it is a natural human feeling and should be honored.

Intimacy goes far beyond sex, but warmth, tenderness, and comfort can aid in allowing you to feel safe enough to share deep feelings with your partner. In this respect, intimacy does not need to have anything to do with lovemaking, but it has everything to do with feeling loved. This can be considered the very core of intimacy.

Creating unconditional love by being completely accepting of your partner is the most intimate you can be. Building the trust that makes you feel safe and secure enough to share unconditional love takes time, and giving that time to each other is the foundation for intimacy.

♡ *Spend an evening talking about how your love for one another has grown since you met and how your partner has made you a better person. Realizing that you have both grown closer and changed because you are a couple can be very intimate.*

Making a Deeper Connection

$\mathcal{T}$o understand how you can create intimacy, even after years without it, let us look at the case of Fred and Ginger. They have been together for fifteen years and have one child. Fred is the owner of his own software company. He is a self-described strong and silent type. His father brought him up to be self-sufficient, the attribute that first attracted Ginger, who works for an advertising agency.

As time passed, Fred's silence and macho attitude began to breed contempt from Ginger, who felt his lack of communication meant he didn't really care for her. This was amplified by his inability to remember her birthday or acknowledge other important events. She said she wanted greater intimacy, which she described as feeling close to someone and sharing emotional growth.

Ginger was aware that Fred's inability to share closeness was not his fault. She was unsure if she was the right person to teach him, and she was angry that he had not grown along with her. She was seriously considering leaving the relationship.

As happens in many relationships, the things that first attracted these two to each other were the same things that later caused them to move away. It was the spiritual quality in Ginger that Fred found stabilizing and inspirational. He felt she would keep him on track in that department and had left his growth up to her. Ginger's desire for a separation came as a surprise to him, but Fred was willing to do whatever it would take to make the relationship work.

Fred and Ginger sought counseling, hoping that the guidance and support would allow Fred to communicate at a deeper level and Ginger to feel she is being heard. Both Fred and Ginger now realize they could have worked harder early on to create the type of intimacy they are now achieving.

When a lack of intimacy has created a chasm, effective communication and a desire to deepen your connection with your partner can be enough to save a relationship. Talk to each other about how you feel; it's the first step to getting what you need and want in relationships.

♡ *Sit down with your partner. Make lists of your needs and desires and how you'd like them fulfilled. Exchange your lists and talk about each other's desires.*

After you have shared your lists, talk about how to meet these needs. Keep your partner's list where you'll see it every day so that their desires will always be at the top of your mind.

When It Gets Too Good

When we fall in love or go through other positive life changes, our old fears of abandonment and insecurities rise to the surface. We worry that our partner will think we're not good enough; we judge ourselves and think we can't do anything right.

New experiences can bring on excitement and anxiety, and sometimes it's hard to tell them apart. It's easy to misunderstand our own feelings. Yet we can choose how to perceive our negative feelings if we understand where they are really coming from.

Negative feelings can come from within us. It happens because we only have so much room in our hearts, and as positive feelings come in, they push out our negative feelings so that we experience them again. The truth is that sometimes judgmental and insecure feelings come from memories of being hurt before. Knowing this gives us a chance to better understand our reactions to both negative and positive feelings.

We all go through changes when love or success enters our lives. There are many stories of how some people seem unable to handle success. Supposedly they fail because they are afraid of success. But the truth is that it is not success that people fear but the changes that accompany success. Success brings with it many changes, and change is difficult. This is where the fear lies.

Take the example of Marge and Homer. They met while working together at a film company. After they had been dating for several months, Homer got a promotion. He told Marge it was her support that got him ahead, but now that he was her boss, he was afraid their relationship might become difficult. Although he cared for her a great deal, he was afraid that maintaining their romance would be too uncomfortable for both of them.

They were both deeply concerned about this. Marge offered to quit her job because she didn't want to lose the relationship. They talked about the various reasons she should stay or go and decided to seek some professional advice.

At their session, Homer shared that he had never experienced so much good stuff in his life. He was afraid something would happen to make it all go away.

Homer wasn't used to having things go his way, and it frightened him. He thought back on how difficult his life had been, how many times he came close to success, only to have it taken away. His superstition that something would go wrong caused him to consider pushing away the love in his life. Together, the couple decided their relationship was the most important thing in their lives and that they wanted to stay together. Marge chose to keep working but to transfer to another department. They both feel fortunate to have each other and good careers, and they vowed never to take their lives and their love for granted.

It has been my experience that it is just as difficult to deal with positive events as it is with negative ones. This is because they both require growth. With negative events, we try to avoid confronting our pain, and thus we avoid growth. When life gets too good, we have no wish to look at what has changed in our lives that brought us to where we are. Why would we want to? It is much easier to kick back and enjoy the sensation.

There may be a feeling of discomfort that we experience when facing the newness of a positive change; this feeling comes from our own lack of self-worth. Understanding this can keep us from misreading what we are really feeling and help us enjoy the gifts life has to offer.

Remember that yesterday is history, tomorrow is a mystery, and today is a gift, which is why we call it the present.

♡ *What things in your life are better than you ever thought they would be? Share with your partner your feelings about where your life is and thank them for helping to create the good stuff.*

Chapter
10

The Need for Nurturing

We are all children, no matter what our age, and need to be nurtured. Caring for someone else comes naturally to most people. Nurturing someone in the way they need to be nurtured, without too much self-sacrifice, is an art form. It requires communication, understanding, and patience.

Letting your loved one know what works is the essence of creating and keeping an emotionally fit relationship.

It may take some practice and patience to create a safe environment for your partner to express their need for nurturance. It may make them feel childlike, and that can be uncomfortable for anyone who works hard at being an adult—and it is hard work. Note that there is a difference between acting childish and childlike. Childish behavior is selfish, manipulative, and demanding, whereas childlike actions may be playful, sensitive, and sometimes tearful.

Nurturing is the ability to be there for your partner when you are needed. It is not a constant state of existence. Both parties must be aware when either role is being overplayed. It is time for a change when you realize you may be caretaking—not allowing your partner to function as an adult and thereby retaining control of the relationship—rather than caregiving, which is caring for someone in a way that empowers you both. A gentle nudge toward reality, by withdrawing some of your caring, may be necessary.

If you are feeling overused in your role, or if your normal relationship seems to have gotten lost, it is your responsibility to tell your partner.

♡   *Try these exercises to help you create more effective and deeper nurturing with your loved ones.*

1.   *Take turns being the giver and receiver over a weekend. Plan to take care of, even pamper, each other. Be sure to share how you like to be taken care of and talk about how it makes you feel.*

2.   *Get in touch with your needs. Share with your partner some of your needs, and then ask your partner how you can best meet their needs.*

Chapter
11

The Case for Marriage

The decision to marry is one that is fraught with numerous factors, including what your parents and friends have done, what you have read, and even your dreams. If you are thinking about marriage your decision also has a lot to do with your age.

Love in your twenties is wonderful. You can talk and make love until dawn, then go to work the next morning. Most people in their twenties don't feel the pressure of the biological clock, either.

In your thirties, the pressure of "it's time to procreate" builds exponentially. For women who have not yet had children and for men who are unsure they want them, you can practically hear the biological clock ticking. Marriage becomes less of a decision of the heart and more of an elimination contest.

In your forties and fifties, the decision can be much more of an emotional one, much more of a choice. You may ask yourself, "Is this the person I want to spend the rest of my life with? Can I imagine being without them? Will my family accept them?" You may also think, "Are they the one? What about my high school crush? Could I do better?" What some people fail to do is remind themselves that they probably have done worse.

Whatever your age, love, and definitely marriage, are a leap of faith. It's a risk, and there's no getting around that. If you have come through some tough times together and been able to be there for each other, it's a very good sign.

You base your decision to marry on your feelings, your prospective partner's behavior, and your mutual goals and desires. A good marriage requires that you enter it with your heart and your eyes wide open. People change as they age, so the more you understand about yourself and your partner's view of life, the easier the process will be. Trust your heart, but don't deny what it is that you know deep within yourself.

If you have questions, ask them. Difficult conversations are the foundation for lasting relationships. The reason most couples don't make it is because they are afraid to lovingly confront their partners with the questions that are gnawing at them. Instead, they hold on to discomfort or emotionally move away, so they don't have to feel. Falling into this trap may be the biggest mistake of your life.

Taking the leap to make your relationship permanent is a scary thing. Remember that anxiety and excitement feel the same in our bodies, so learn to tell the difference. Your excitement about marriage is natural, and so are the moments of fear every couple experiences as they take that long walk to the altar.

♡ *If you are feeling uncertain about whether your relationship is moving in the direction of marriage, here are some steps to take.*

1. *If you don't think you want to get married, and you know your partner does, it's time to put your cards on the table. Although it may be painful, you need to tell the whole truth about how you feel about marriage.*

2. *If you are waiting for your partner to ask you to marry them and you've been together for more than a couple of years, chances are it's not going to happen. Either pop the question yourself, or ask them how they really feel about taking that stroll down the aisle.*

The Nature of Attraction

Mutual attraction is one of the keys to a healthy relationship. It has a lot less to do with the way you look than you might think.

People are biochemically attracted to each other. Attraction is an internal process that can be enhanced by stimulating the five senses, but it has more to do with our own biochemistry than anything else. It's how you affect another person. Other people are mirrors for our internal feelings. They will reflect back to us what we are putting out.

When we are depressed, we are far less attractive to others. Even the most physically beautiful people are not attractive when they are in bad moods. A positive attitude is your most exciting attribute. We all know people who are less than physically perfect but have wonderful and fulfilling relationships. I believe that their inner joy is what allows them to attract and keep good partners.

There are two different types of attraction. The first is sexual attraction. You are probably familiar with this feeling; you walk into a room and see someone who makes your heart beat faster. There is a reason for this feeling; it is your DNA talking to their DNA and saying we could make a baby. It insures survival of the species. It has its place, and without this feeling, many great poems and love songs would never have been written.

Sexual attraction is inspirational. It also is a type of temporary insanity. By its nature, sexual attraction can be a selfish type of love because your own needs are always the first thing considered.

The second and more positive type of attraction is spiritual attraction. Generally, when we meet someone we are spiritually attracted to, we feel close to them very quickly. We tend to want these people in our lives because they fill many of our deeper needs.

When we are immature, we keep searching for the sexual type of love and can sometimes overlook people who may be able to fill our hearts and souls. Partners who truly love us, who are truly there for us, make our world a much more wonderful place to be. Sexual attraction between two people who also have a spiritual attraction is passionate, loving, and fulfilling. It goes far beyond any fantasy. It is far superior to being with a person who just fills our sexual needs and leaves the rest of our inner being to wither. When the entire self is loved, the sexual experience becomes transcendental, and this moves us into new realms that can include increased energy, heightened creativity, and greater depth of feeling.

If you are finding that you are feeling less attractive to your partner, a simple change of routine may be in order. Eating the same food every day is boring; being with someone who acts the same way out of habit is also unexciting. Variety can be an attractive element in any relationship. It is easy to change the daily routine and add a little spice into your relationship, but don't try something you can't easily pull off.

♡ *Here are two exercises designed to assist you in discovering your inner attraction: Mirror exercises like the first one are great fun, but may take a little getting used to.*

1. *Look into the mirror and tell yourself that you are beautiful. If you feel uncomfortable when you do this, it's a sign that the exercise is working. Each time you tell yourself that you're beautiful, you build your self-esteem and reflect on your inner beauty. Every time you look into a mirror, look for the reflection of your soul.*

2. *Sit with your partner and explain what first attracted you to them. Ask your partner to do the same about you. You can then talk about what you now find attractive about each other.*

The Importance of Touch

In a relationship, touching each other is one of the most powerful forms of communication. Touch heals and provides emotional sustenance.

Numerous studies have revealed that infants who were not touched daily failed to thrive. Do you know that some elderly people who live alone actually go to medical doctors so that another human being will touch them?

We don't touch enough in America. In a study done by Dr. Sidney Gerrard, he found that people in Puerto Rico touched an average of 180 times a day and people in France touched about 110 times a day (so much for the French being the most romantic). Now guess how those numbers compare to how much we touch in our country.

The average American couple touches only two times a day, and yes, this does include sex.

These statistics actually shocked me. I'm a toucher and am fortunate enough to be with a loving woman who is also a toucher. The combination of a toucher and a nontoucher is one of the most difficult relationships to have because neither partner has a deep emotional understanding of what the other person needs. The touching partner usually feels unfilled, abandoned, and hurt, while the nontouching partner cannot understand why they are making such a big deal about it. The nontoucher sometimes says things like, "I touch you every time we have sex, don't I?"

If you haven't figured it out yet, touching only when you have sex is not nearly enough, and it makes the neglected partner feel hurt and angry. When we get angry, we don't want to be touched, and we can get into an uncomfortable dance of touch me, don't touch me, but please touch me. It is painful. If you love your partner but don't touch them outside the bedroom, there may be some low-grade anger in both of you that needs to be looked at.

If you are not naturally a toucher, perhaps because you were brought up in a nontouching household, you need to get out of your box. This may feel uncomfortable at first, but I have seen many instances where a nontoucher has become a can't-get-enough type in a very short time.

♡ *Here are some practical exercises to help you and your partner get in touch.*

1. *Since the dawn of humanity, touch has been one of the greatest gifts in our very short lives. Hold the person you love tightly, and feel your hearts touch. It is the closest thing to heaven that we have on earth.*

2. *Couples caught up in the nontouching merry-go-round need to put the brakes on and get off.... And I mean right now. Hold your partner's face in your hands, or just hold their hand. Let them feel your fingers against the small of their back or their shoulder when you pass by them in the house. Kiss them gently, in a nonsexual way, so they can feel the unconditional part of your love for them.*

3. *People who aren't naturally touchy may not know how to appropriately touch you in the way you like. If your partner needs help, show them how and where you like to be caressed and touched.*

Go to Bed Together

*N*o one really knows what happens when we sleep. Oh sure, there is a lot of scientific data about theta and delta brain waves, REMs and dreams. But something else happens to a couple when they lie next to each other every night for several hours. I believe that some kind of emotional energy is exchanged and it creates a closeness that goes far deeper than lovemaking. Sleeping together is one of the most important parts of a relationship.

Couples who have widely divergent hours can find it difficult to sleep together, but the successful ones have found ways to make it work. Take the example of Jack and Jackie. Jackie runs a company and wakes at 5:30 A.M. so she likes to be in bed by 8:30 P.M. This is way too early for Jack, who is a business consultant and gets his best ideas late into the evening. They have managed their differing hours by incorporating a very simple method.

They always go to bed together. No matter how early or late, they have agreed that it is important to their relationship that they lie next to each other at the end of the day. Lovemaking is always an option but not a requirement. Their goal is to connect before she falls asleep; after she does, Jack either stays in bed to read or write, or gets up and watches TV or plays with the dogs.

This isn't some confusing control issue for either one of them. They have both accepted that bonding in this way most every evening brings them together and keeps them close, and I agree. Going to bed together and lying in each other's arms, even if it's only for twenty minutes or so, is a great way to connect and share a nonverbal "I love you."

People who travel extensively or whose loved ones are away for long periods of time usually say that, while they do miss sex, they mostly miss the holding and the moments where they touch in the middle of the night. The point is that being in bed together keeps the relationship connected in ways that no other activity can.

Couples who are having difficulties often avoid this kind of contact, which only creates a deeper separation and less intimacy. One of the best tools a struggling couple can use to get closer is to go to bed at the same time and just snuggle.

Going to bed together is one of the most valuable and accessible tools a couple can use to stay connected for the long haul. Even if you've had words and are angry with each other, agree to drop it when you reach the bedroom door.

♡ *Here are some new bedtime activities to try out.*

1. *Develop your own bedtime ritual together such as snuggling up, reading from a favorite book together, or just watching TV while lying in each other's arms or playing footsies.*

2. *Before you go to sleep, tell your partner, "I'll see you in my dreams." Even if this doesn't happen, the idea alone is enough to make your partner feel loved.*

3. *Turn off the television fifteen minutes before you go to sleep; spend that time just holding each other. This kind of intimacy creates a deep connection and will enhance your relationship and your lives together.*

Ten Tips to Increase Intimacy

C ouples in intimate relationships have some things in common. Much of the time it's not about what they do or don't do; it's about who they are as people and how they behave with each other.

Here are some of the many ways the happiest of couples interact with each other. Try them out.

1. Be best friends.

Tom Hanks and Steven Spielberg both say that their wives are their best friends. People who think that having a best friend as a partner is unromantic are usually single and bitter. Having a best friend in your heart and bed is the best part of a loving relationship.

2. *Be able to laugh at yourselves.*

Maintaining a sense of humor about your life and your relationship is one of the keys to thriving. Life can throw many curves and without the ability to see and appreciate the irony, you could end up hating the world and each other.

3. *Be open to new ideas and experiences.*

If your partner only wanted to do the things you like to do, life would soon become dull and uninteresting. Having a partner who exposes you to different perspectives and dreams will make your world and soul fulfilled.

4. *Be willing to be willing.*

When change or compromise is called for, you don't have to accept it immediately. Just being willing to look at things from another perspective can often be enough to help you resolve most differences that occur in an emotionally fit relationship.

5. Be kind.

Kindness and courtesy are perhaps the most undervalued and underused of human virtues. Courtesy, communication, and kindness can turn conflict into consensus.

6. Be able to give all of your attention.

Giving your partner 100 percent of your attention when they want to talk to you is one of the most bonding and powerful things you can do. Put down the remote control or whatever you're reading, face your partner, and say, "What would you like to talk about?" It will make your partner feel loved and important.

7. Be demonstrative.

Couples who often touch and hold each other often have fewer arguments, enjoy life more, and stay healthier. Touching is one of the deepest forms of communication. See chapter 13 for more tips on touching.

8. Be trustworthy.

Never give your partner any reason to doubt your loyalty or devotion. Whenever you are away from each other, check in regularly to let your partner know you're okay.

9. *Be available.*

If your partner has a problem, be the one they call first. Commitment means that you can count on your partner to be there for you when you need them.

10. *Be proactive.*

Couples who take a relationship inventory and see what they have as well as what it is they might need in the future, are much better prepared for difficulty and have longer lasting, more successful relationships.

PART
3

Romance

The Secret to Romance Is In the Bag

The last time I was buying a gift for my partner at Victoria's Secret, the girl behind the counter said, "You're great. Some guys just don't get it."

As I walked into the elevator with my two large pink-and-white-striped bags, I had the feeling that the three women on the elevator were staring at me.

No sooner did the doors close when one of them said, "Are those all for you?" I immediately responded, "No, they're for her."

"Does she know how wonderful you are?" asked another woman, holding the hand of her daughter. "She tells me everyday," I said, praying for the doors to open. How long does it take to go one floor anyway?

The third woman chimed in, "Good, because we all want to take you home." And the doors parted. Like Moses crossing the Red Sea, I bravely walked through the mall to the parking lot. Men must not get it, I thought. Why else would these women respond so openly?

As I got to my car, a couple—well actually the female part of the couple—noticed me putting the bags away. She said to me, "Look at you, with those Victoria's Secret bags. Bet you're not married, are you? Married men don't do stuff like that."

"Yes, I am, and yes they do," I said, wanting to defend married men in general and her husband in particular.

I think men are romantic by nature. Now stop laughing. The problem is that they don't know where to go for new ideas when they run out of their own. Feeling romantic is easy. Figuring out what to do to create a little more romance in your relationship is the hard part.

The important thing is to know that when you feel romantic, if you don't do something romantic, you won't get to be romantic. You have to keep romance alive throughout your lives by saying and doing the little things.

♡ *Romance is a state of mind, not an act. If you want to express your romantic feelings to someone you love, do something, anything, rather than nothing. Remember,* when it comes to romance, it's the deeds that count. Here are some ideas to get started.

1. Talk about what each of you finds romantic. You might be pleasantly surprised that your partner has some creative ideas for romance.

2. Make a romance "wish list" that you exchange with your partner and one night a week grant each other's wishes.

3. Much of romance is making the effort. For example, a single flower can have as much of an effect as a dozen roses. When it comes to romantic gestures, something is almost always better than nothing.

Romantic Memories

*E*very now and then an opportunity arises that would be both wonderfully romantic and create a great memory. Sometimes we push aside these opportunities because work and life may seem overwhelming and seizing the romantic moment can be daunting. I suggest you think twice before letting a beautiful experience vanish. As we look back on our lives, we connect the years through significant events. Creating a wonderful and romantic memory is a marker for your lives as a couple and family.

Some of these events evolve from romantic moments into rituals, further strengthening the tie that binds you together. Many couples are actually unaware of how their little daily rituals make them a stronger couple. I know of one woman who said that when times were tough, it was the fact that her husband brought her coffee in bed every morning that made her hang in there.

Another couple I observed had a unique ritual: when either of them had an itchy nose, one or the other commented that it meant he or she was going to be "kissed by a fool," and they would kiss each other. It may seem silly, but it's these little things that create a big connection.

The next time you take a vacation, let the idea that you are creating romantic memories together make the adventure a little bit sweeter. And when you return from work each day and say, "Hi honey, I'm home," know that this is one of the little romantic rituals that speaks to your heart and says, "This is the person I belong with."

♡ *Think of yourself as being on a romantic scavenger hunt. Any time you can put a romantic spin on a daily task do it. Also, try some of these exercises.*

1. *If you have difficulty thinking of any obvious rituals or any significant romantic memories that you have shared, don't be discouraged. These things can be subtle. Spend a little time observing yourself and your partner, and talk about the most important moments you have had.*

2. *Any time you're in a store and see some little thing that you know your partner would like, get it for them. Once you each get into the habit, it will become*

a part of your relationship and will help you both create the kind of love that will last forever.

3. Another good and very simple thing to do is to make a life/relationship map. Take a large sheet of paper and draw a horizontal line all the way across it. Make the line at the beginning, to signify when you first met, and then mark other points along the line to indicate the important moments of your life together. Most couples who engage in this exercise find that they have many more romantic memories than they realized and the exercise itself (which also counts) helps them see how important their time together really is.

4. Write each other a letter with a favorite romantic memory, describing how you felt when it was happening, and how it makes you feel to remember it. This little "love note" will become a treasured keepsake and remind you of your romantic memories for years to come.

The Romantic Connection

*E*veryone in a relationship wants to feel romantically connected. We have all had times when our partners call us just as we pick up the phone to call them or says exactly what we were going to say just then. These romantic connections are common among couples who have spent a good deal of time together. They also occur with couples who are just naturally in tune with each other.

When we first meet someone that we have intense feelings for, we may experience this type of romantic connection. Some people mistake this experience as a sign of true love. While it is true that deeply connected people share each other's thoughts on a more regular basis, when it happens with a new relationship it does not necessarily mean that you are meant to be together. Only time will tell.

A wonderful romantic connection can also intimidate couples, whether they have just met or have been together for ages. Especially private people may resent someone else being the voice inside their heads. Others may thrive on the connection so much that their partners are uncomfortable by their desire to be so close. But most people receive a deep sense of comfort knowing that they are in tune and romantically connected with their partners.

A loss or absence of romantic connection can signify a lack of balance in a relationship. It can also make you aware that your partner may be going through a difficult time. If you are concerned, talk to your partner about it and trust that they will see your questions as an act of bonding, not an inquisition.

To strengthen a romantic connection, you need to become more aware of its existence. Listen to your intuitive or gut feelings and express them. When your partner has said something you were just thinking, tell them. The more you become aware of these feelings and the more you verbalize them, the stronger your relationship will become.

♡ *Here are some other ideas for developing a deeper connection.*

1. *Write a special note to your partner proclaiming your love. This is a gift of the heart, which is always a winner.*

2. *Sometimes it's scary to be creative. It's important, listen to your heart. What would your partner truly appreciate? It doesn't have to be wildly complicated or expensive. What about taking your partner to a movie you normally wouldn't pick? A man might like to have his partner with him while a secret agent detonates special effects. For most women, holding their partner's hand while watching a love story is terribly romantic.*

Ten Tips to Enhance Romance

Creating magical moments in your relationship is something everyone thinks about but few people do. Perhaps it's because they actually can't think of exactly what to do. Taking the time to create romance in your relationship is paramount to creating a fulfilling love life. Even if you think your ideas are silly, your partner will be thrilled that you took the time to do something loving for them.

Here are ten acts of love that you can do with and for your partner to bring more romance into your relationship. Don't try to do everything on this list in the same weekend; doing one a month is plenty. These ideas are just a little help to get you started.

1. *Date your mate.*

Plan a night out every week. Make the reservations and get dressed up. This is something that you can both look forward to all week long.

2. *Make the time at the end of the workday when you first see one another extra special by giving each other a ten-second hug and kiss.*

You will both feel more deeply connected throughout the evening. Also remember to touch your partner affectionately throughout the day, not just when you want to be romantic. See chapter 13.

3. *Take time to make time.*

Plan a romantic rendezvous during the week. You can get a room at a local hotel or plan to have the house all to yourselves. Just the anticipation of being together in this way will add spark to your romantic life.

4. *Make your mornings special by bringing your partner a cup of coffee while they are still in bed.*

   You can also serve them breakfast in bed. It will make your partner feel cherished, and they will return the kindness.

5. *Take the time to tell your partner that they look wonderful, beautiful, sexy or great.*

   We all have doubts about our looks, and telling your partner that they are attractive helps to create a romantic relationship. See chapter 49.

6. *Before you leave in the morning, tell your partner that you are looking forward to seeing them when you return.*

   Never leave the house without acknowledging your partner or saying, "I love you."

7. *Next time you are shopping alone, get a couple of little gifts for your partner.*

   The next time he or she is feeling down, give them one of the gifts as a surprise. This is a wonderful and uplifting act of love and will be remembered for a very long time.

8. *If your partner is having a rough day, offer to take them out or make dinner for them.*

   If they are the one who usually does the cooking, this will come as a welcome change and a sign of your appreciation. If they are experiencing stress at work, it will be a great way for them to unwind from a tough day.

9. *Rent a convertible and kidnap your partner for a drive to a romantic spot.*

   This is a wonderful and simple thing to do. If you want to be a little more extravagant, you can choose to spend the night at a bed-and-breakfast and drive home the next day.

10. *This one is terribly romantic, so don't try it unless you're ready for a passionate evening.*

    Get your partner two or more roses. Take one of them and pull off the petals. Drop the petals on the floor leading to the bedroom and place several petals on the bed. Put the other roses in a vase on the nightstand. Your partner will never forget your thoughtfulness.

PART 4

Sex

Sex Is an All-Day Affair

In order for a relationship to be truly sexually intimate, affection has to be exchanged throughout the day. Have coffee together in the morning, talk on the phone during the day and on your way home, exchange e-mails, and greet your partner at the door. I always suggest that couples who are apart during the day share a deep ten-second kiss when they see each other again. These all help to build intimacy and enhance your love life.

Most people want their sex life to be hot and intimate, and it all starts by letting your partner know that this is what you want. Take time for what's most important—being together. Put the bills, housework, and phone calls to the side once in a while.

There are dozens of ways to liven up your sex life, but don't overlook the simple things that turned you on when you were in high school. Try giving your partner some favorite perfume or cologne to reawaken the smells of those horny by-gone days. By the way, our noses play a very important role in sex. Never underestimate how smelling great (or bad) can affect your love life.

Lastly, don't let the passage of time make you doubt the value of this special connection. Most experts agree that sex can get better and better as time passes and intimacy increases. Mature couples also report that, though sex is less frequent than it was in years past, it is still fun, often more satisfying, and it enhances their ability to enjoy life. The stability of a long-term relationship helps to create a healthy sex life because it's difficult to freeze out a person you are intimately and sexually attached to.

♡ *Here are some ways to enhance your sex life.*

1. *Intercourse is obviously a large portion of sex, but it is only one part. Kissing, touching, or gazing into each other's eyes are also very important in the sexual quotient. Even innuendo help make your love life sexier. Think of being romantic as the appetizer to a full-course meal. Then have some foreplay as your entrée, and do the wild thing for dessert.*

2. *Try making out on the sofa before going to bed, experiment with having sex in different places, or in different ways. Remember that intimacy is built on a bedrock of trust, so always be conscious of your partner's comfort level, which is what makes a person feel safe enough to be sexually open.*

3. *Ask your partner what smells turn them on and let them know what you like as well.*

4. *A regular sexual connection is extremely important to a successful relationship. Have sex at least once a week. Even if you're not in the mood when you start, you'll get there in ten minutes.*

Let's Talk About Sex

Sexual incompatibility is one of the major reasons couples become emotionally distant and split up. It can start out simply, like one partner wanting sex more often than the other does. Sometimes a person rejects a partner out of anger, and other times there are just greatly divergent styles and tastes.

Yet finding a middle ground and avoiding incompatibility is not that tough. One of the most common problem that couples have is that they seldom, if ever, talk about sex. If couples actually talked about their sex lives, there would be less infidelity, fewer arguments, and fewer bedtime headaches.

Couples have to find a way to create a safe space to discuss sex. If sex is a subject that you think will "take care of itself," and you don't think that you need to discuss it, think again. A good rule of thumb is that when something makes you squirm, it desperately needs to come out in conversation.

Once you start the discussion, you may be surprised to discover it's not that difficult to find a balance. It may be as simple as agreeing to make love a little more often than you want it and a little less often than they want it, or vice versa.

Let's look at what a committed relationship really means. If you have vowed not to go anywhere else for sex, then your partner should understand and return the commitment. In other words, you need to be available to each other sexually because you've promised not to go anywhere else for it.

This does not mean you have to submit to your partner at the drop of a hat. Again, it's a matter of discussing what the correct balance is for your relationship. For example, if your partner is not feeling well or if your needs are extreme, then you must come to terms with what's best for both of you.

It's easy to become selfish when it comes to sex; it's also easy to use withholding as a means of control. Being sexually frustrated makes people feel badly about themselves and usually emerges as anger toward the rejecting partner in some way. This will only create discord and discomfort in what should be one of the most comforting and enjoyable parts of your life.

Understanding that our sexual patterns go through different stages as a relationship matures may help you to deal with that issue, as well. In the beginning, sex is very exciting, and then, as you grow together, it becomes sweet and loving. Not appreciating the sweetness because you miss the excitement is detrimental.

♡ *When I was in high school, the saying was, those who talked about sex never did it. What I have learned from my years in practice is that, in loving relationships, those who never talk about sex don't do it either.*

1. *Creating excitement is something you can easily do, but only if you're willing to talk about it. Handing your partner a videotape and saying, "Let's do it this way" isn't exactly communicating about sex. If you need something more or different, sit down and have a conversation about it. If you cannot summon up the courage to discuss this very human process, invest some time and talk with a therapist.*

2. *It comes as a surprise to many people that it's okay to just pleasure your partner. If for any reason you're not into "it," taking care of your partner is a loving thing to do, and there are many ways to do it without intercourse. Some couples use touching and kissing to please their lovers and maintain a healthy sexual exchange. Be creative.*

Chapter
22

Sex, Desire, and Boundaries

Not everything feels good to everybody. Sometimes our partners can unknowingly make us feel uncomfortable or even unsafe. Our sexual desires and comfort levels change as we mature. These desires can broaden, or they can become more conservative. No one should judge or be judged by what makes them feel comfortable or good in bed.

We all give hints to what we want and don't want in our sexual relationships, but many times, hints are not enough. If your sexual boundaries are being crossed or your desires are not being fulfilled, you must find a way to communicate that to your partner. If you do not tell them, your resentment will build and eventually restrict your enjoyment of lovemaking.

Finding a time and a way of telling your partner may feel scary. If you remember that your partner loves you and wants to please you, it will make talking easier. Most people are receptive to knowing what pleases their partner. For truly loving and sensitive couples, pleasing their partner is the most important and most fulfilling part of the sexual experience.

One of the most common problems associated with lovemaking is timing. If your partner has had a bad day, the idea of sex may be the last thing on their mind. If you can be understanding and just hold them, you will nurture your romantic relationship through the long run.

When sexual incompatibility becomes a greater issue than a couple can deal with, it may help to go to a professional. There are many excellent therapists specializing in sexual issues. There are also many books and DVDs on the subject. Michele Weiner-Davis and Albert Ellis are two of the most famous sexperts in the world. Both have several books and videos that are widely available.

One of the most common problems that people experience is lack of sexual desire. Luckily, sexual desire is not just a spontaneous feeling or something that once lost can never again be found. It does require effort and patience, but if both parties are willing, the process of reawakening sexual desire can be very fulfilling and exciting. Remember, the only reason not to make love is if it doesn't feel good afterward.

Unfortunately, sometimes it is not the desire for sex that is missing but the desire for your partner that has diminished. Resentment is often the cause.

One way to overcome this dilemma is to try to let go of your anger appropriately. Anger taken to bed often becomes a tool for destructive sexual behavior. Withholding, violence, and a lack of enjoyment are just a few of the outcomes that can come from going to bed angry. If necessary, you can agree to disagree and continue your discussion the next morning. Do your best to leave anger at the bedroom door.

Understanding your boundaries, limitations, and desires, as well as your partner's, is a great way to assure that you will have a healthy and happy sex life. If you have issues here, don't procrastinate; most sexual issues don't get better with time.

♡ *Communication is the key to unlocking hidden desires and a wonderful gift. Don't go to bed without it.*

1. *If you want to put the spark back into your love life, don't wait for the mood to come over you. If you act romantic, you will feel romantic. Start by setting the scene: Light candles, take a bubble bath, have a little champagne, dress sexy. Once you create a romantic stage, playing the part becomes natural and usually unavoidable.*

2. *Make a list of things that you want to try sexually, things you're curious about but a little afraid of, and share them with your partner.*

3. *If you haven't ever told your partner what it is that turns you on, now is the time. To make it easier, share this chapter with him or her.*

Rekindle the Fire

$\mathcal{W}$hen we first fall in love, we constantly think of the other person and try to spend much of our time in romantic situations. This courtship period is based on sexual attraction and infatuation, but it is also a time when mutual interests develop and we establish the foundation for a long-term relationship.

Unfortunately, the sensation of romantic love seldom seems to last. When it wanes, feelings of caring, comfort, and commitment take its place. These feelings are powerful enough to support a loving relationship and can continue throughout a lifetime.

Sometimes, however, these deeper emotions do not give you everything you need to continue to be satisfied with your relationship. You may be discontented or bored with "married sex" and may fantasize about different ways of having sex or even different partners. This is natural human behavior and so common that former President Jimmy Carter even shared his very personal feelings with the world by saying that he lusted after other women ... in his heart. It's normal to become a little bored with sex in a committed relationship of many years—unless you get creative.

Many people feel a tremendous amount of guilt about their natural needs and desires and hold back these feelings from their partners. Couples who learn to encourage each other to be open about what they would like sexually have much less difficulty in coping with these normal human challenges.

It's also fine to be creative. If watching a movie with a sexy actor or actress makes you aroused, using that spark to create a little romance is perfectly fine. On the other hand, having an "emotional affair" or maintaining a friendship with someone who totally turns you on can be very destructive. It's best if the "other people" in your fantasy life are imaginary or unattainable.

There are numerous other ways to put the fire back into your relationship. Many books, videos, and classes are available to help with this pleasant task. Take some time to check out the vast amount of material available to help you relight the fire in your relationship. You will find it to be one of the most rewarding and pleasurable investments of your life.

♡ *Sometimes you just have to get into it before you can get into it. So, I say, "Just do it and see what happens." A dry spell can last for years if you let it. Try one of these tips to get things started.*

1. One of the sexiest things you can do with your partner is to tell him or her that you want to make your love life better. Be sure to do this in a fun and uplifting way; shaming someone about sex can damage their desire to do it.

2. Unplug the TV and leave a note on the remote and TV saying, "Turn me on instead."

3. Write a sexy love note to your partner and insert it in the book they are reading.

4. Don't just walk into the house as usual. Pause on the porch, ring the doorbell, and greet your partner with a red rose and a bottle of champagne.

Ten Tips to Ignite the Sexual Fires

*W*e all admire couples who seem to have found the secret to keeping their sexual fires burning. Luckily, there are many ways to relight the torch. It just takes a little energy.

When trying to heal a relationship or even give it a sexual tune-up, one of the most difficult things to do is to figure out just what to do. To aid you in that quest, here is a list of my top ten tips for adding some fuel to your fire.

1. *Act sexy and you'll feel sexy.*

   Play the part by setting the scene with candle-light and soft music, softer words, lingerie, and great smells. This creates a fanciful mood for both of you, and sex will be unavoidable.

2. *Make your bedroom a romantic hideaway.*

   Get some silk sheets and soft lights. Having a place to go when the feelings come over you is important to keeping romance alive.

3. *Talk about sex.*

   Call your partner in the middle of the day and tell them you can't wait to make love to them. Drop little sexual innuendoes and talk about sex. Conversations about love may be one of the most underrated aphrodisiacs. See chapter 21 for more ideas.

4. *Share your secret romantic fantasy with your partner and ask them to tell you theirs.*

   Then make plans to play your fantasies out. Just the anticipation will add to your romance, and the gift of giving each other what you desire will be something that you will never forget. See chapter 23.

5. Make love at least once a week.

This may be the most important and most disregarded rule of sexual intimacy. Connecting in this way is something that both of you can look forward to all week long as your special time together.

6. Be creative.

Relive your first encounter, kidnap your partner for a weekend getaway, have chocolate-covered strawberries and champagne in bed, or serenade your partner with your favorite song. There are so many different ways to be sexy. Just go with your ideas (or buy a book to get some). It's really hard to do it wrong.

7. Kiss often.

Couples who kiss every day make love more than those who don't. One of the sexiest things you can do with your partner is to just spend a night making out and cuddling.

8. Let go.

Give your partner total control in the physical romance department every once in a while. It's surprising how they will surprise you if they can give to you in any way they want. There is also something freeing about giving up control. Just say to the one you love, "Honey, I'm all yours. Do with me what you will."

9. Compliment each other.

Everyone wants to know they're desirable, and we all wonder if our partners still find us sexy after a few years have gone by. Compliments should take place throughout the day. This way, at bedtime, your partner will already feel desired and you will reap the benefits.

10. Think about sex.

We all think about sex, but sometimes we forget to put our partner in the picture with us. Next time your mind wanders in that direction, be sure to focus on being with the person you love. See chapter 20.

PART 5

Keeping

Your

Balance

Happiness Is an Inside Job

Has your partner ever blamed you for their unhappiness? Have you ever blamed your partner for your unhappiness? In a loving relationship, your partner's happiness, hard as it is to believe, is not your responsibility. Sometimes our loved ones may try to make us responsible for the lack of joy in their lives, but doing so reflects misguided thinking. By doing this, they are depriving themselves of any chance to find real fulfillment.

If we feel that making our partner happy is our responsibility, then we have created an impossible task for ourselves. We cannot make someone else feel happy; they must learn to do this for themselves.

Even if you succeed in making your partner happy, you may have had to sacrifice your own happiness in the process. Trying to make your partner happy at any expense is a setup for resentment. Eventually you lose the ability to give to them and to yourself.

Happiness means different things to different people. Some people may not even know what it is that makes them happy. For others, their pain is so great that nothing can get beyond it. The first step to helping someone to discover happiness is to be there for them when they need to share their feelings. As the sadness leaves, it will create a space that can be filled by happiness and love. One of the greatest gifts we can give to our partners is to let them discover that they are responsible for their own happiness.

Take the example of Chandler and Monica. Married for seven years, they have a four-year old son, Joey. Recently, Monica realized that she has allowed Chandler to control her by making her responsible for his happiness. Anything that went wrong in their lives was her fault. Monica took on his blame and it wore away at her self-esteem. Though Monica was quite aware, she couldn't seem to let go of the need to be a people pleaser.

When they realized how deeply rooted their codependent behavior was, they both joined support groups. In their separate groups, they are becoming more aware of how they can be a better couple as well as better parents and people. After each of their support groups meets, they talk about issues and share their feelings with each other.

Understanding the nature of their problem was the beginning for them. It is a difficult path, but they are both seeing the results of what they are doing. Their commitment to work on themselves and find their own happiness is the bond that will hold them together.

I tell clients "Happiness is not an exit on the freeway. It is not a place you can ever get to. You have to find it where you are right now." By sharing your feelings, questions, and ideas with those you love, you will discover new ways of creating joy and enjoying the life you have. Only then will you find happiness, as Dorothy said when she returned from Oz, "in your own backyard."

♡ *Here are some ideas for finding happiness.*

1. *A simple way to develop happiness is to keep a gratitude journal. Every night, list five things you are grateful for and read them every morning when you wake up. Within two weeks, your attitude will become more positive. This little exercise really works, and anyone can do it.*

2. *Many times we don't actually know what makes us happy. Ask your partner what things they see that make you happy. Having a mirror to reflect the joys of life is a gift.*

3. *Make a list of what you need to be happy. Just think about the things that make you smile, jump up and down, or cause you to say "Yes!"*

Finding Emotional Balance

If a relationship is the most important aspect of your life, then you may be putting too much emphasis on it. Like a balloon with too much air, it will eventually explode.

A relationship should never be your entire life. It's only part of a whole. Work, growth, and creativity are also important. No one thing should take over to the exclusion of the others.

We all know people who have nothing in their lives but their work. This may bring them financial success, but they may have no friends, few creative outlets, and may never have deep relationships. When couples focus entirely on each other, they don't allow themselves the freedom to grow and create. When the relationship goes from the primary focus to the only focus, other things that life has to offer are lost.

Although I believe a person can grow more within a relationship than without one, I also believe it is necessary to find a balance between self and other. If you are consumed with a relationship, it may be a good idea to dial your energy back a little bit and look for other things in life that are also fulfilling.

Dialing back will serve two purposes. It will make you more attractive to your partner, and it will open up new areas of creativity. If you continue to put pressure on the relationship, you will either lose the joy in it or, worse, lose the relationship altogether.

Take the example of Luke and Laura. For two years, they've been talking about moving in together and getting married, but Laura doesn't feel comfortable committing to this plan, even though Luke is supporting her and her son from a previous marriage.

Instead of dialing back, Luke keeps putting on the pressure, trying to find ways to get Laura to accept the kind of relationship he envisions. His frustration increased when he attended the wedding of two friends and realized he is the only unmarried member of his family.

He even tried to talk Laura into moving to the country, so she could focus all her attention on him. He told her his plan was for her to assist him in his business. Convinced that all this is the right thing for both of them, Luke keeps giving Laura the hard sell and then feels disappointed when she continues to resist.

In truth, Luke is trying to control Laura and trying to control the course of their relationship. His relentless pressure for a commitment and his "let's do it now" focus is actually pushing her away—to the point where she may never find the emotional space to accept his idea of a dream life. What he needs to do now is to slowdown and let things happen in their own time.

As a therapist, I like the idea that we are all born with a gift and it is our job in life to find out how to share it with the world. Being consumed with a relationship gets in the way of doing this important work. Time alone can help us discover what life is all about.

♡ *These exercises may help you if you are overly focused on your relationship:*

1. *Do something for yourself that doesn't involve your partner: Take a short trip, visit an old friend, clean out your desk. The point here is to rediscover that you have a life apart from your partner and to discover new parts of yourself.*

2. *Write down your feelings about the relationship situation instead of avoiding them. Once feelings are on paper, they can be dealt with.*

3. *Write down your personal desires, plans, expectations, and fantasies. Don't omit anything.*

4. *Make a conscious choice to spend an entire weekend alone. Take the telephone off the hook, lock the door, and unplug the TV.*

We All Need Time Alone

When you are in a loving relationship and you have a desire for time alone, a normal human requirement, it's common to feel uncomfortable. There is an obvious fear about sharing this need with your partner, who may misunderstand and whose feelings may be hurt. The two of you must develop an understanding that time alone does not threaten your relationship and is not a form of punishment or avoidance. If it is not easy to talk about, it may be because one of you is insecure about some aspect of your relationship.

Constantly needing to be with your partner is a sign of enmeshment and is usually based on insecurity. Even if you were brought up with the idea that you should constantly be together, it may not work for your relationship.

The fact is that everyone needs some space sometimes. This is not to say that one or the other of you can't get lonely or feel insecure. You need to develop security and trust if any kind of significant alone time is to work in your lives. Begin by acknowledging that each of you has the need to be on your own from time to time. You must trust each other not to abuse this understanding.

Being in a relationship with someone who can give you the space you need is a very comforting feeling. Just knowing you have the option is sometimes enough; you may not need to exercise it. When the need for space is acute, try to talk about it as soon as possible. Both of you need to discuss your feelings; talking will help and most likely make the need for space less urgent.

♡ *Giving space may take some practice. Here are some exercises that will help you to integrate this into your life.*

1. *Go on an outing together, to a museum, for instance. When you get there, you may both want to see different things. Go your separate ways and meet in a couple of hours to share what each of you has seen.*

2. *If you don't think taking separate vacations is an appropriate idea (and I don't), go together but plan one or two separate side trips. Always share what you did.*

3. *Create your own space in the house. It can be a work area, a hobby space or even a closet, as long as it is yours.*

4. *Try sitting in front of a fire together, each reading your own book. In this way, you have allowed yourself and your partner to be where you want to be while still being together.*

Pay Attention to Emotional Needs

Dealing appropriately with your own emotions can be difficult. Dealing appropriately with your partner's emotions is an art form. To help each other deal with feelings, you must do your best to understand and get comfortable with the fact that someone else's feelings may not have a great deal to do with you. Life, work, physical well-being, friends, and family can all be sources of strong emotions; taking it personally will not allow you to stay objective.

The first step for dealing successfully with difficult feelings is to do your best to not be judgmental when either of you is being emotional. Feelings don't need to be justified; they need to be honored.

Being there for your partner while they feel emotional is very effective in helping the feelings heal. Looking at feelings and acknowledging them is the next step in dealing with them. Strange as it may seem, just admitting something doesn't feel right will give you a sense of control in what might seem like an out-of-control world.

Be supportive and encourage your partner to talk, and you talk too. Together you will find balance, and the difficult emotions will give way to calm faster than if you tried to ignore them.

Also, remember emotions can be harmful if you choose to act out irrationally. If you know that you or your partner's emotions are running high, make sure you avoid any temptation to say or do hurtful things. If you find you cannot control yourself or you have no patience with your loved one, it is time to seek help.

Lastly, unhealed emotions drain your energy and ability to deal with your relationship. The more emotions are repressed, the worse they can become. Do your best to not let unhealed emotions run your life; use good communication skills to share your feelings rationally. These tried-and-true tools are as much common sense as they are psychotherapeutic. They'll help you deal with the normal range of emotions that make their way into most relationships.

♡ *Understand that feelings are a good thing—if you deal with them. Taking action when you have emotions will bring more peace into your life. Try doing these exercises.*

1. *Letting your partner download their emotions is a wonderful gift and will help your relationship grow. The next time the one you love is having strong feelings about something (even if it's you) tell them it's okay to tell you all about it—then just listen.*

2. *You don't always need to talk. Sometimes just a hug or a kiss will help someone cope with powerful feelings.*

3. *Share a kind word or two. It may give your partner just the boost they need.*

Encountering Change

*E*ncountering change within relationships, even very small changes, can create incredible anxiety. You may feel that all of the rules that you have lived by are suddenly thrown out. When old rules no longer work, people can feel helpless, abandoned, or out of control. This can create a great deal of fear and anger and can even cause destructive behavior.

The first step in dealing with change is to find the source of your discomfort. Examine yourself and talk with your partner. Try to identify and write down some of what you are feeling. This will make your emotions clearer and give you a starting point to begin a gentle discussion of what needs to change. Remember to keep an eye on how the discussion is making you feel and what other emotions are coming to light.

In all relationships, we naturally grow and change, and so do our dreams. The changes we make are often conscious choices or willing sacrifices. One example is setting aside the dream of playing in a rock band to hold down a good job and raise a family, another is choosing to work as a legal secretary so you can have more time with your children rather than leading the life of a high-powered attorney. These are conscious choices; each can also be described as a willing sacrifice.

It's also possible to suddenly wake up one day and not recognize the person you have become. At that point, the choices you've made may seem more like unwilling sacrifices. This may lead you to blame your partner for not allowing you to follow your original dreams. You can resolve that inner conflict if you can recognize that you have made conscious choices along the way.

Raising children, dealing with financial frustrations, and planning for retirement are examples of what most people see as reasons for making changes. What we often fail to see is that change is a natural process that comes as our relationships, spirits, and bodies mature. Partners need to be mirrors for one other, to identify the changes that are needed in order to secure future happiness. Couples who can do this are able to share their complete selves as their relationships grow.

Change has been described as the only constant in the universe. If you are afraid of change, or simply don't want to make changes, it could be a sign of deeper issues that need to be healed. Take charge of your life and your relationship and brave through the changes. In this case, it will give you back much more energy than you put in.

♡ *Create a contingency plan. Knowing what to do if something catastrophic were to happen will ease your fears. Have a discussion with your partner and write down how you or your mate would cope with a disaster like an injury or job loss.*

Think Before You Act

In your relationship, have you ever felt the tension is so thick you could cut it with a knife?

As adults, we may feel that there is no need for our partner or anyone else to tell us how to behave. If we have an issue with our partner, we sometimes believe that we don't have to approach them and deal directly with the problem.

Many couples have difficulty expressing their feelings appropriately to each other because they may feel that it's a sign of failure. On the contrary, it's a sign that you really care.

Other couples don't communicate about problems because they don't have an easy method for doing so. Here is a three-step methodology that is a nonthreatening way to communicate and create harmony and respect in your relationship.

First, take the time to think before you act. If you don't believe this is important, remember how an inappropriate comment, note, or email can affect your mood and behavior.

Ask yourself:

1. What am I after?

2. Am I part of the problem?

3. Am I trying to cast blame?

4. Is there old stuff I am using to fuel this fire?

5. How did this all get started?

6. Am I just trying to win?

7. Am I in the right frame of mind to deal appropriately with this person/situation?

8. What will happen if I just let it be?

9. What will happen if I try to take control?

10. What is the best thing for all concerned?

Second, after you have considered some of the questions above, if you still feel the issue is relevant, take a moment and consider how to present it to your partner. Just dropping your troubles and concerns in their lap when they are totally unprepared will only create a new issue and the issue you really needed to talk about will get left behind.

Third, consider what action you need to take, and where and when you could take that action. Also remember that no action is still an action.

If you are the one to whom an issue is being presented, please remember that there is only one appropriate initial response. Say, "Thank you for bringing this to my attention." This will instantly make your partner feel that you are open to hearing them, and there will be much less tension around the issue and in the air.

♡ *Problems happen daily. It's how we receive and resolve them that separate the successful couples from the rest.*

1. *Discuss your fears about fighting and reassure each other that just because you fight doesn't mean you don't care. (Note: This is never an excuse for verbal abuse.)*

2. *Come up with an olive branch, such as a particular joke you share, or some body language or act that indicates the fight is over. You can offer to make your partner a cup of coffee or take them out for ice cream. Make it easy for both of you.*

Ten Tips for Relationship Satisfaction

*U*nderstanding your need to feel satisfied in your relationship and answering to that need will make both of you happier people.

If you are not feeling satisfied in your relationship, these ten tips could help you achieve that very important goal.

1. Recognize each other for your commitment and caring.

The number one motivator of people is recognition. Letting someone you love know how they have added to your life is one of the highest compliments they can receive. See chapter 2 for more on how to show you care.

2. *Share in creating a positive and emotionally comfortable living environment.*
Love cannot thrive in a negative environment. Keeping it positive helps everyone in the household (even your cat) enjoy their lives more.

3. *Make your relationship meaningful.*
Work together to create something worthwhile. Whether it's contributing to your community, your faith, or the world, doing it as a couple will add depth and a sense of higher purpose to your relationship.

4. *Be responsible for your actions.*
If you make a mistake, own up to it sooner rather than later and always do it completely. This gets it out of the way and allows easier healing because the problem has had no time to fester and grow. See chapter 8 for more on the importance of communication.

5. *Be accountable for your commitments.*

When you make a promise, keep it. If you break your word, your partner may have difficulty believing you will be there next time.

6. *Balance the work and the rewards.*

Trade off household duties every now and then; it will help you and your partner feel you are in a balanced relationship. If you are in a partnership where one of you works and the other takes care of the home and children, you need to make sure the stay-at-home partner has equal access to the household income. See chapter 32.

7. *Help each other to grow and learn.*

Encourage your partner to be open to new experiences. People who are not growing do not feel good about themselves, and this will cause them to feel they are bringing less into their relationship.

8. *Give your partner the opportunity to be their best.*

When you know that your partner takes pride in certain tasks or endeavors, support them in succeeding at those things. Remember that greatness in any one area leads to greatness in all areas.

9. *Understand your partner's motivation and stresses.*

If you know that your partner has difficulty talking with the accountant, dealing with the phone company, or performing other tasks of living, take on that responsibility. If your partner responds to certain forms of kindness or affection, offer those gifts. See chapter 10 for more tips on nurturing your partner.

10. *Keep it interesting.*

Do nice things for no reason. Greet your partner with enthusiasm when you see them at the end of the day, and keep some spontaneity in the relationship.

PART 6

Resolving

Life's

Problems

Income and Incompatibility

Incompatibility in many relationships can be reduced to its first two syllables ... income. When your lifestyle is threatened or drastically altered because of financial changes, it can affect your relationship. When our insecurity buttons are pushed, we tend to overreact.

Remember, the state of the economy is not your fault. Also remember that you have the ability to change your situation. If you communicate your feelings to your partner, the chances of your relationship surviving what is almost always a temporary situation will be greatly increased.

If you start slowly, work hard, get help, and do not expect significant changes overnight, the financial difficulties should pass. It will help to remember that this is something the two of you are working through together. If you support each other and talk about what you're feeling, you will not only survive, you will thrive. Here's an example of how one couple did it.

When Fred and Ethel met, they were both working. Their individual successes were attractive elements for both of them. When they married and had a child, Ethel decided to stop working and be a stay-at-home mom. They both agreed this was best for their child. Fred was doing well in his new career. He felt confident he could take care of his family. They bought a home and made several thousand dollars' worth of improvements. Their family and relationship grew.

Shortly thereafter, Fred's business took a substantial loss. It was a struggle to pay the bills, and Ethel found out she was pregnant again.

Fred grew stressed. He felt overwhelmed and wanted some help. Ethel was also upset because their social position was now different. Making do with less money was new and uncomfortable for her. Her family offered some help, but Fred's pride would not permit him to accept their gifts. They argued over little things that had nothing to do with what was really bothering them. Luckily, after getting some counseling, they realized that this was the only life they would have, and they needed to focus on the positive and make the best of it. They committed to get through their financial downturn together. They reminded each other that what was most important to them was not lifestyle but being a loving family. That was the true meaning of their lives.

♡ *Talking about money is important. Arguing about it is a signal that your fears are running your life. Try these exercises for a great investment in your relationship.*

1. *Make discussions about finances a part of your relationship process; communicating about the business side of a relationship is necessary to help both of you find balance and feel secure.*

2. *Another way of helping both of you deal with your current financial differences is to examine how you were brought up. How our families dealt with money has a lot to do with our own financial styles.*

3. *Talk about your attitudes toward money in a relationship and marriage. Do you feel that after you're married all the money is ours? If you do and your partner doesn't, it's time to get things sorted out.*

4. *If you have waited too long to try to bring up the topic of money, then getting started can create uncomfortable feelings. You will simply have to ignore your discomfort and dive right in. If you choose to see a counselor specializing in financial issues for couples, make sure the person you see is licensed and experienced. Many helpful books and Web sites on the subject are also available.*

We Grow by Solving Problems

Almost everyone has a desire to avoid problems. We will go to almost any length to avert pain. In many cases, the energy we spend avoiding pain is much greater than what we would use in facing it. What we fail to realize is that through problem solving, we grow. When we view our problems as challenges that make up our lives and face them head on, we also could save endless hours of frustration.

One thing you can count on is that as soon as one problem is solved, another will come in to take its place. As overwhelming as this can sound, the greater truth here is that each time we deal with difficulty, we learn for the next time. It's when we struggle to avoid the difficulties that we stagnate. That's why so many couples seem to stay in the same emotional place for a long time.

One of the benefits of being in a loving relationship is that you have a partner, a mirror, to help you solve your difficulties. Even if you are dealing with a relationship problem, your partner may be able to help you solve it. If you both work to resolve the difficulty, the pain decreases, and both of you learn form the experience.

If you choose not to work on your problems, they will increase and begin to consume your every waking moment. People who fail to face life's difficulties are always running. They never seem to find any time or reason to be happy.

There are times in any relationship when problems seem to gang up on a couple. Unforeseen crises will inevitably arise. Couples who survive these misfortunes are able to summon up emotional resources, some from previous experiences. They also are able to understand why each problem arose, which helps them avoid similar ones in the future.

Our capacity for solving problems is greatly increased if we are aware that we have room in our lives for change. If a couple is rigid in their beliefs and encounters a problem that is not within their belief structure, it can break their relationship. The couple that keeps on searching and reevaluating their problems will not only find the answers they seek, they will grow in the process.

The most important thing to remember is that blaming your partner for problems is the quickest way to end the relationship. We all make mistakes. A couple must agree to work out the difficulties that arise together, as a team. If you solve your problems together, without blame, your relationship will flourish.

The challenges we face in our daily lives are what make us better people and better partners in a relationship. Problems only become overwhelming when we feel we don't have support. Let your partner know you are open to hearing whatever is troubling them. Your emotional support will give both of you the strength you need to see the issues with greater clarity.

♡ *Make time to have a problem-solving session, at which both you and your partner sit down to look at where you and your problems stand. Take a blank sheet of paper and list your problems in order of difficulty. Take care of the hardest ones first. This will make each successful problem-solving session easier. With both of you working on your individual as well as your relationship problems, you will feel supported. This will also make the process much easier.*

How to Deal with Being Apart

Separations are hard on any relationship. Absences do not make the heart grow fonder if they are too long or too numerous. In relationships where one partner travels a great deal, or where career or family obligations require extended absences, you need to examine and talk about the difficulties of separation before someone has to leave.

The prospect of a long separation may bring up fears about life without your loved one, and you need to discuss your feelings of abandonment. Taking the time to allow both of you to talk about your feelings will help diffuse some of the difficulty.

I cannot overemphasize the importance of having this discussion before someone leaves. Your talk should not be about logistics or money matters. It should focus on the emotional aspects of how you will feel while your partner is away. Beginning the conversation with talk of practical issues may be a good way to get started, but make sure to give the emotional component its due.

Do not be surprised if feelings of anger surface. Some people use anger as a means of releasing fear and/or sadness. Give each other the room to let the feelings flow. Once the surface feelings are out, the deeper issues can be shared in a loving way.

For those who can communicate regularly, phone calls and e-mails can make a long separation easier. For many in the military, this is impossible and there is the additional fear of serious injury or even death. For the loved one who's at home, anxiety may become a part of daily life, and you will need to find ways to get support from family and friends.

If your loved one can't contact you or is not easy to reach, you can still write or e-mail them daily. Do not be concerned that they may not be getting your correspondence in a timely manner. When they do receive your communications, they will take delight in the fact that you took time out every day to think of them and send your love. This will also help you deal with the pain of separation, because it puts you in touch with your feelings more often.

When your loved one is away, it's never wise to air grievances or try to resolve unhealed issues. This is the time to be supportive of each other and trust that there will be an opportunity to deal with those matters when your loved one returns.

Understanding, accepting, and dealing with your feelings about the separation is a gift to everyone involved. If you have the need for additional aid, there are numerous support groups and counselors available. The best thing you can do for someone who is far away is to find a way to be strong for them.

♡ *Taking the following steps will help you cope with separation.*

1. *Make a plan for how to communicate during your partner's absence. Discuss what your emotional needs may be.*

2. *If you call your loved one, and they're not available, be sure to leave a loving message. Don't just hang up or say you'll call back.*

3. *Make a plan to think of each other at a specific time of day. Sometimes just knowing that your partner is thinking of you is a big plus. Be sure to take into account time-zone changes and daily activities. Those couple of minutes can become a very important part of your day and will enhance the feeling that you and your loved one are still deeply connected.*

4. *If you can't communicate directly, keep a journal and share it with your partner when you see each other again.*

Invalidation, a Subtle Form of Abuse

Invalidation is where one person directly or indirectly discounts the feelings or actions of another. If invalidation is one of the challenges you face in your relationship, understanding why a person behaves this way can help you to overcome this uncomfortable problem.

Poor experience with past relationships can be a reason for this behavior. People who invalidate their friends and loved ones can often feel inferior to them, or they may be holding on to resentments from the past.

Ask yourself who was the best person you ever knew and why. This should be your role model for how you treat others and for how you need others to treat you. Now ask yourself, who was the most difficult person you ever knew and note their behaviors. If you or your family members act in any of these ways, you need to stop. These behaviors cause people to feel invalidated.

It is sometimes difficult to identify invalidation, because the methods are often very subtle. Invalidating behavior ranges from very obvious to covert and can be conscious or subconscious.

People slip into this type of behavior when triggered by past traumas. If someone you care about is treating you poorly, you can ask them if there is anything going on in their lives that may be causing them to feel badly about themselves. Shedding some light on their triggers may help them curtail their behavior.

Invalidation is a great way to avoid responsibility for a situation and to make the invalidator feel better about themself. Invalidators use a variety of methods, including building you up only to bring you down, cutting you off, and projecting their own feelings onto you. They also use generalizing, double messages and double binding, which is where you are "damned if you do and damned if you don't."

To have successful relationships, you need to find ways to heal the damage that has been done and to find ways to eliminate invalidation from your life. To do this effectively, you need to examine and perhaps remove some things from your communications, including generalizations, insults, blame, accusations, engaging in arguments, judging, righteousness, and making it personal.

Negative behaviors and invalidation can be counteracted by a number of methods, including being empathic, being respectful and patient, using diplomacy, staying present for the whole conversation, listening, and taking a break if things get overheated. Sticking to and firmly repeating the facts is a powerful way to destroy invalidation. Also, asking people to repeat an invalidation can defuse it, as most invalidations are insinuations, vocal inflections, and double messages that can be replaced with the simple truth.

Maintaining boundaries by saying no, setting limits, and describing what you can do is helpful when dealing with someone who is using pressure, demands, or manipulation to get what they want.

Sometimes people have gotten away with this type of behavior for so long that it has become a habit, and they may not know they are doing it. If invalidation has become the norm for you or your loved ones, it is time to seek some guidance. Eliminating invalidation completely from your life is not possible. However, to be able to contain it and to empower yourself and your family to solve these problems will directly add joy and healing to your life.

♡ *Here are some ways to keep invalidation at bay.*

1. *Discuss what you find invalidating (a tone of voice, a dismissive comment, a joke at the wrong moment, sarcasm, body language). This way your partner can avoid these behaviors.*

2. Create a plan to signal your partner when something invalidating has occurred. You need to agree that upon receiving the signal the behavior needs to stop and a counterbalance needs to take place ASAP.

3. Invalidation only gets worse as time goes on, so don't let it slide. It's important to talk about it. Exploring the intent helps to reduce invalidation. To do this, try asking, "When you said that, what were you really trying to say?"

Forgiveness

To err is human, but very few of us are divine, and forgiveness can be a difficult task. If your partner has been all too human and made a mistake, forgiving can mean the difference between success and failure in your relationship. Many times, we choose not to forgive our loved ones as a means of punishing them. In truth, we may only be punishing ourselves.

If your partner has transgressed in such a way that you think you couldn't ever trust them again, and you are thinking you may have to leave your relationship, think again. Everyone makes mistakes; in fact, everyone makes big mistakes at some time in their lives. If you and your partner are the type of people who want to grow in your lives and your relationship, you can learn from this and make your relationship even stronger. If you want to forgive them—and realize this may take some time—stay in the relationship and work on it.

Once again, communication is the key. Creating a safe space to talk about your feelings is paramount. Even though this may be uncomfortable, the process will bring you closer together and help to build an understanding that will put your entire relationship on a more positive path.

In order to get on with your lives, you must begin by telling each other the whole truth. Share all of the facts and feelings that led up to this difficulty. In the process of sharing your feelings, consciously refrain from blame and judgment. Allow the flow of feelings to continue until you have expressed and exhausted all of your emotions.

It may take time to get to the root of your feelings. The process of doing this kind of communication can be overwhelming for even the most conscious and loving partners. It might be wise to have an objective third party available to keep you on track. Sometimes finding the right words and keeping emotions in check can be very difficult.

Forgiveness is perhaps the most healing act you can bestow on yourself and your partner. Holding on to resentment and anger is very destructive to your sense of well-being. Many medical professionals believe that this kind of stress can lead to disease. It's worth letting go of negative feelings and getting on with your life rather than holding on to emotions that can kill you. Being able to forgive is the action of an aware human being. It is healthy, loving, and even somewhat divine.

♡ *Here is an exercise in forgiveness to help you let go of negative feelings and make your life a better place to be. Try doing it at least once a year—how about on New Year's Day or your anniversary?*

1. *First, make a list of all the resentments you are holding toward your partner, including the big one. Do this to help to release your negative feelings.*

2. *Next, write a letter to your partner saying that you forgive them and are releasing the negative feelings. In this letter, share your desire for both of you to understand the cause of the actions and to move forward with your lives. As you sign the letter, see yourself releasing your anger.*

3. *Read the letter out loud several times to yourself, and if you're comfortable, to a friend or therapist. With each reading, see yourself letting go of the pain. When you feel you have fully let go, you may then share the letter with your partner.*

4. *Lastly, as a symbol of releasing, both of you should burn the letter and watch the pain of the past go up in smoke.*

Loss Is a Teacher

All people, no matter how strong, enlightened, or loved, have to deal with the pain of loss and change in their lives. The task of confronting feelings of grief is difficult and requires a great deal of energy. The experience is often exhausting, and time seems to·stand still or pass rapidly before your eyes.

At these times, facing other people, even those you truly love, can be tough. Sometimes you may want to run and hide. Loss can cause you to reorganize your priorities, and you may not perform normal tasks up to your usual level. The process changes you; it also changes how you relate to other people.

This is the time when you need to take greater care of yourself. This may be hard for your loved one to understand.

They may feel that you are pulling away from them or that they have been unable to meet your needs in some way. It is important to remind them that this is your personal process and though their presence is comforting they cannot take away your pain.

We all must learn to allow our grief to heal in its own time. Our partners need to give us, as we need to give ourselves, room to do things differently.

The most important thing is that you honor your feelings. Allowing the pain to heal in its own time is a valuable step in caring for yourself.

There are five stages to the grieving process: denial, anger, bargaining, depression, and acceptance. People do not necessarily go through these stages one at a time or in any particular order (with the exception of acceptance which, most of the time, happens last).

Acknowledging your partner's pain, by honoring their feelings and encouraging them to heal, is a way of showing them your love. Understanding your loved one may be difficult. The fluctuating of feelings and the frustration you may feel as you try to help is part of the process. If you remember to stay open to communication and support your partner's personal grieving process, their pain will end and your relationship will have grown.

Perhaps the most difficult situation that a couple can face is when they are both grieving a tragedy such as the loss of a child. This is one of the most painful experiences anyone can go through. At times like these, it is very important that both people seek support from counselors, clergy, and family. Without this support, the relationship can be burdened past its breaking point.

If this most unfortunate crisis has occurred in your lives, seek help immediately. There are many organizations and support groups available in local communities and online, ready to provide assistance. Elisabeth Kubler-Ross, whose groundbreaking book *On Death and Dying* is a great source of understanding and comfort, offers the Web site www.elisa bethkublerross.com, with excellent resources and referrals.

If we feel our pain fully and allow ourselves to grieve completely, we can travel through life without the excess baggage of unfinished business. We need to move through our denial and accept where we are.

♡ *Healing our hearts and feeling love again has to do with acceptance and forgiveness. Once we have been through the grieving process, our lives are changed forever. It teaches us the meaning of life and the value of the people who we love and who love us. Try the following exercises to help you prepare for loss.*

1. *Discuss how you feel about loss and what you have done (or need to do) in order to help heal the pain.*

2. *Tell your partner how they can best support you when a significant loss occurs.*

3. *Constructively release your anger by exercising, writing, or talking with your partner about it.*

Ten Tips for Resolving Conflicts

Every couple argues. Some do it overtly by yelling at each other while others do it covertly by avoiding contact and conversation. Whatever the method, the result is the same—hurt feelings and disenchantment.

Here are my tips to help you resolve conflicts constructively. If done correctly, resolving conflict can be a pathway to growth and problem solving. Research has shown that couples who are in conflict more than twenty percent of the time are probably not going to survive. Hopefully, these tips will help you get your arguments under control and reduce the level of energy in those arguments.

1. *Understand that anger itself is not destructive.*

   There is a vast difference between anger and rage. When someone is angry, they need to state their feelings. They don't break things or relationships. That is rageful behavior.

2. *Talk about your feelings before you get angry.*

   When you or your partner can approach the situation as it happens and deal with it in a safe way, it may not get to the point of being an argument. Sometimes you just need to verbalize things and most arguments can be avoided if your partner understands how you feel. See chapter 47.

3. *Don't raise your voice.*

   It's amazing how issues of hurt feelings or differences can be resolved with a whisper. I counsel couples who are yellers to only communicate with a whisper, and it greatly reduces the anger in their relationships.

4. *Don't threaten your relationship and don't take every argument as a threat to your relationship.*

   This type of emotional blackmail puts the other partner in a panic/flight-or-flight mode. While you're telling them you want to leave, they may be making plans to find a roommate. In addition, they may be so devastated by the thought of losing their family, they can go into a deep depression and be unable to give you what you need.

5. *Don't stockpile.*

   This is where you bring up issues from the past to use as a hammer against whatever problem your partner has asked for help with. Deal with their issue first, and if you really have unresolved feelings from past problems, talk about them another time. See chapter 40.

6. *Don't avoid your anger.*

   If you stuff your feelings long enough, you will explode and say or do things that you will regret. Anger does not diminish love; you can be angry with those you love. In fact, the ones we love hurt us the most because we love them the most.

7. Create a process for resolving problems without anger.

Start by each of you taking five minutes to state your feelings. Then take a twenty-minute break and come back to the table for another ten minutes to discuss how you think you can best deal with the problem. Also, know that it's okay if the problem doesn't get solved right away. See chapter 48.

8. Don't ever allow abuse.

This includes verbal abuse or any type of violence including slamming doors, breaking plates, or hitting. If your arguments escalate to this level, you need to leave the house. If one partner ever hits another a police report needs to be made by the victim and an appointment with a therapist is mandatory for the perpetrator.

9. Don't engage in argument.

Remember that negative attention is still attention. If your partner tries to goad you into an argument, simply don't go there. Some people actually like to argue because it gives them a temporary feeling of power and gratification. Avoid being sucked into their need for attention. See chapter 31.

10. *Listen to your body.*

When you are angry, your body releases chemicals that may cause you to react in ways that can be destructive to you, your partner and your relationship. Learn to understand your feelings and how the process of anger affects you physically and emotionally.

Pain, Hurt, and Anger

Is It Hurt or Anger?

*M*any people do not want to feel sadness. If they are unable or unwilling to feel their own pain, what comes out instead are angry feelings and words, and the target is usually someone they love. The difference between anger and other feelings is that when you're angry, you may have the impulse to hurt others. In order to heal, it helps to understand that the basis of most anger is some kind of deep resentment at being hurt.

We all have a responsibility to take care of ourselves without hurting those we love. As bizarre as it sounds, sometimes we want to hurt the ones we love because they are the ones that can hurt us the most. I have heard couples in therapy say to each other, "The reason I hate you so much is because I love you so much."

Anger comes in overt (an obvious display) and covert (passive-aggressive) forms. One way that covert anger hurts us is by subconsciously directing us to relive old painful memories. For example, if a woman has been hurt or ridiculed by her father or her brother and doesn't deal with it, she will find a man who will treat her the same way because she unconsciously thinks that if she can change him, it will heal a lifetime of hurt.

In relationships, covert anger hurts the ones we love because when a person is being distant or withdrawn, their partner feels it. If you pull away from your partner, it hurts them. Behavior that may seem selfish can, in time, shatter the foundation of a loving relationship.

If you release anger in an unconscious or passive-aggressive way (like being continually late for dinner or not responding to your partner romantically), you don't really let it out. Unfortunately, adults can turn their rage inward and act it out with some form of covert anger.

It's actually healing to tell someone you love how you really feel, rather than holding it inside. It's much more comfortable than lying to yourself or trying to manipulate your partner. You are living a dishonest relationship when no one realizes what the real feelings are, and relationships can't survive in a sea of dishonesty.

If your partner is withholding affection and attention, you need to let them know that you understand that they are angry and that you are willing to discuss it and are willing to make appropriate changes if necessary. People have a responsibility to deal with their deepest, darkest feelings in a secure manner. If you or your partner are holding on to or expressing anger inappropriately, talk about it.

Emotional release is essential to good health. If you are feeling sad, you need to cry. If you're feeling angry, you need to express the anger but in a constructive way. If you don't get in touch with what you're really feeling, you may express the emotion you are most comfortable with, the one that you think gives you control.

Trying to express yourself or control others with rage is the most unproductive tactic anyone can take when trying to resolve discord. The raging person may feel a temporary release of emotion, but their partner is left feeling horrible and hurt. Rage may win the battle, but you could lose your relationship in the process.

Take the example of Clark and Lois, who have been together for more than three years. They have been talking about marriage, but Lois is reluctant. Her unavailability angers Clark. The discussion usually ends in a big argument, and they have had several temporary breakups. They have been doing this same dance for more than six months, and they both feel unsupported and misunderstood.

When they have these arguments, Lois feels that Clark is threatening her. She fears she can't trust him and worries about his ability to stick with the relationship during the rough times. This, in turn, raises fears of abandonment and reminds her of past losses. Lois also resents Clark for trying to control her by frightening her.

Clark enjoys letting his anger out. Once he emotes, he feels much better. Lois had a father who raged, as did her ex-husband, so rage is not something she wants in her marriage. Even though Clark knows all of this, he doesn't feel he needs to change his style of fighting; he believes his anger is justified.

Although he doesn't want to lose her, Clark cannot seem to back off when things get heated. He wants to go ahead with their plans to marry or else end the relationship. He feels rejected while she feels threatened.

Clark needs to stop trying to be like Superman and learn to be Empathyman. If he were able to feel and understand Lois's pain and talk with her calmly, he could then come to her rescue. Clark needs to let go of his anger and change his communication style in order to allow some trust to build in the relationship.

We all experience hurt, but expressing pain can be embarrassing and uncomfortable, so some people express anger instead. Rage can momentarily feel good, as it (temporarily) makes us feel powerful, but it doesn't really work in the long run. If we mistakenly project this anger on to our partner in life—the person who is there to help us deal with our feelings—and we scare them away, what are we left with? Perhaps no one. So, it's better to express feelings appropriately, rather than "letting them have it." Releasing anger in that way, to the person we love, is a hurtful act and it never helps resolve a disagreement.

If you can't talk about a topic without the conversation escalating into a fight, you need to see a qualified therapist. The therapist's job is to create a safe place for their clients to express their feelings and explore their destructive impulses without hurting anyone.

A final note: If there is any sign of violence, you must protect yourself and your loved ones by getting help, even if that means calling the police. This may be scary because of the possible repercussions, but the alternative can be a lot more devastating. There are a number of anger management programs available, and most mental health clinics or county health facilities can direct you to one.

♡ *Here are some tips for expressing anger appropriately.*

1. *When we have multiple emotions occurring, or when we bypass our pain, it can be easy to forget who we are talking to and release our anger inappropriately. To stay focused, develop a sense of appreciation for your partner and what they are saying to you at the moment. Forget about everything else except why you love your partner and why you are together. It only takes a second and it changes your whole point of view. When you consciously say to yourself, "This is the person I love," it makes a big difference in how you communicate with each other.*

2. *If you are a person who spends a nanosecond feeling hurt and then goes straight to anger, check in with yourself the next time you get mad. Your best way of healing is to talk about the pain, not act out the anger.*

3. Write a letter to your partner about how you (or they) went to anger instead of feeling the pain. Don't blame or shame the other person. Use "I statements," so they don't feel attacked.

Fighting Fair

*I*n every relationship, there are going to be arguments. Most people do not realize these altercations can have positive as well as negative outcomes. The reason for the argument may be silly, such as the age-old toothpaste tube debate. The difficulty is not in why you disagree but in how you conduct the argument.

Some couples can actually make light of their difficulties. Archie and Edith Bunker come to mind. As difficult as Archie was to live with, Edith was able, gently and jokingly, to put him in his place. Unfortunately, there are numerous couples who cannot argue constructively or who cannot make light of their own difficulties, and they resort to unfair fighting.

There are several different styles of unfair fighting, including the silent treatment, the heated retort, and being a bully. None of these styles works.

The silent treatment gets you nowhere because it hides what you are feeling. A heated retort may release excess energy and surface anger, but most of the time, the release becomes a bigger deal than the reason behind it. This is one of the ways that small disagreements can escalate into big fights.

Perhaps the most inappropriate style of fighting is being the bully, when one person intimidates the other by yelling, name-calling, or threatening to leave the relationship. It is not fair or productive to fight in this manner. It will take a relationship down and eventually out.

Some people like to fight. They like the adrenaline rush and find it empowering. After they have released their anger, they feel relaxed and even loving. Their partner is usually left feeling confused, abused, and violated.

It is not fair for one person to take advantage of another in order to gain control or self-satisfaction. If this type of behavior is familiar to you, then your relationship and perhaps your physical well-being are in danger.

Both of you need to understand how to deal with this destructive kind of communication. It can be dealt with constructively, providing both of you agree to work through the process.

Unresolved anger has a way of sneaking up on you when you least expect it, and it will escalate problems rather than erase them. Some people hold on to old pain from past relationships, and without realizing what they are doing, express inappropriate anger at their partner. If you think this is something you may have done, examine it carefully so as not to allow it to happen again.

If you think of the heart as a vessel, it's easy to understand that it can only hold a limited amount of feeling. When filled with anger and resentment, there is no room for love to come in. You have to learn to release anger appropriately to be able to love more completely.

Whole hearts don't require negative feelings to fill them up. To have a secure relationship, you have to learn how to make each other feel safe, even while you argue. If your style of arguing creates distance and fear, you have to learn a new way of communicating your upsets.

♡ *Here are two tips to help you release your anger appropriately and to learn to fight fair.*

1. *A great way to help each other feel safe and to preserve your relationship is to argue with respect. Never threaten the relationship (or your partner) and don't call each other names or belittle each other. Couples who fight respectfully are much more likely to stay together.*

2. *Remember to never go to bed angry. If there has been a difficulty between the two of you, work it out before you go to sleep or agree to disagree and put it aside for the night. In the morning, you may see things in a new light.*

Artistic Apology

$\mathcal{E}$ach of us has said the wrong thing at the wrong time. Sometimes it embarrasses us. When we try to cover up our embarrassment with righteous indignation, a real problem can begin.

The truth is, to resolve the problem, we have to take responsibility for creating the energy that caused the upset, and that can be difficult.

Sometimes when we have said the wrong thing and have hurt someone we care for, we really can believe that we were helpless to prevent it. We may feel that we were provoked. Some of us have been conditioned to cast blame.

To understand this in yourself, there are two issues to consider. First, where does this tendency to blame come from? For example, did you come from a family of blamers, or is blame prevalent in your work life? If so, then you may have learned that this kind of projection is reasonable. Second, are you willing to assume the role of a victim in your adult life? You have the choice to cast away any thoughts of blame. No one can make you feel any particular way. To let go of the roles you know and choose a new experience is sometimes the wisest choice to make, but it's never easy.

To avoid reinforcing false beliefs that someone other than yourself is responsible for your behavior, don't wait to make amends after you first realize that you have said the wrong thing. Don't let time pass. Stop and apologize. Waiting too long to remedy the situation can cause resentments to build in your relationship.

If you are behaving a certain way because you feel unappreciated, then you need to appreciate yourself. If it's been a hard day, then you need to learn to ask for compassion—not snarl, grumble and try to make your partner feel as bad as you do. That creates a win-lose scenario rather than a win-win situation.

If you feel your partner has said something that was hurtful, it is appropriate to take immediate action and respond. The correct method is to look at your partner and say directly that what was said has hurt you and you would like your partner to stop the behavior and talk about why it has occurred.

It's not necessary to get an immediate apology. Some people need a little time to process their feelings. An hour is the average time it takes for most people to calm down and realize what it is they need to do. If much more time is necessary, or if days go by without the two of you speaking, it's time to discuss the matter with a third party.

Sometimes the ego, in its effort to protect people, makes apologizing difficult. Saying you are sorry or being willing to admit you've been wrong can be one of the hardest things to do. If you have made a mistake, then put your pride aside and ask for forgiveness.

On the other hand, if you feel you are the wronged party, be sure you are not holding a grudge that can prevent you from opening up and accepting an apology from your partner. No matter how willing your partner may be to say they are sorry, it cannot work unless you are willing to accept it.

If your goal is to punish your partner rather than to get on with your life, you really need to reconsider your motivation. Relationships are designed for individual growth as well as companionship, and growing requires acceptance and forgiveness.

In most cases, you only have to make an apology once. There is no need to say "I'm sorry" over and over again. If your partner is demanding this from you, then it's their issue, not yours. If this is happening in your relationship, your partner may need to have you always be in the wrong, which is a way of keeping control in the relationship.

If you say you're sorry too often and too easily, you will seem insincere, and this will create distrust and distance in your relationship. People sometimes resort to this tactic when they just want to placate their partner and don't really want to change their own behavior. It also happens when someone feels like the underdog, wanting to be told, "It's okay." Look at an apology as a sacred act and not something you hand out like Halloween candy. It is hard to maintain your self-worth if you feel you need to make an apology too often.

When couples can find a way to resolve their disagreements completely, they form the basis to solve their other issues rationally and lovingly. Their making up is sincere because they don't hold on to the past.

Learning how to make up has to start somewhere, and it's always best to begin at the beginning. You both need to acknowledge the problem, state your feelings, and then, if appropriate, make your apology. That's really all it takes. If your partner doesn't have other issues, they will be willing to accept your apology and move forward.

♡ *Taking responsibility for mistaken words and doing what is necessary to correct the situation is a sign of maturity. Besides making you feel good about yourself and strengthening your character, it will strengthen your relationship. Here are some ideas to get started.*

1. *Talk with your partner about a time when you wanted to apologize but didn't, and use this moment to say you're sorry. It will make your next apology much easier.*

2. *If either one of you is holding on to a memory of saying the wrong thing, talk about it now so you can finally let it go.*

3. *Discuss how apologies were (or were not) made in your families of origin. This will give you greater insight into each other's behavior.*

Taming the Green-Eyed Monster

Most of us have experienced the uncomfortable feeling of jealousy, which can be sexually, materially, or even emotionally oriented. The type of jealousy or its manner of expression is not as important as how it arises, and most often, jealousy comes from a lack of honest communication.

Unfortunately, most of the time, feelings of jealousy are born out of insecurity and low self-esteem. You can choose to live with it, act it out inappropriately, or get over it.

People who believe in themselves rarely feel jealous. They know that the world is abundant, and that there is enough love to go around. They are happy when they are by themselves and know that they will have a full life even if their partners are not with them. Their lives aren't run by the fear of not getting what they want or losing what they have.

To get past feelings of jealousy, you need to do two things. First, be aware of it. That will make it easier to deal with. Second, talk to your partner about it, so you can quell any mistaken ideas you may have.

Being with your partner may bring up feelings you experienced in your family of origin or in previous relationships. If a parent or an old love made you feel not good enough, certain things your partner does may remind you of those feelings. Sometimes you may feel that you don't deserve the good that you've gotten in your life and fear that it will be taken away. Unhealed experiences can become the seeds of doubt that cause jealousy.

This example will help you better understand how jealous feelings come about.

Robin and Marian had been living together for three years when they came to therapy to discuss their jealousy problem. Marian is a corporate vice-president in her mid-thirties, and is anxious to marry and start a family. Robin is in his mid-forties and owns a graphic arts company. Ninety percent of his staff is women, which makes Marian uncomfortable.

Whenever one of Robin's female staff members would call, Marian would grill him with questions about his interest in the woman. She would want to know if he had plans to see her outside of work and if the woman was in a relationship or single. If Robin had an interview with a woman, the first words out of Marian's mouth were, "Is she attractive?"

Marian's insecurity escalated to the point where she became jealous of every woman Robin ever knew or worked with. Although she could not admit it, it was obvious to both Robin and Marian that on some level she did not trust Robin, even though she believed that he was faithful to her.

Robin began to feel that he could not share parts of his life with Marian because she would react with suspicion. Her insecurity and jealousy was very difficult for him to handle; it both hurt and angered him.

In therapy, it came to light that Marian's father had cheated on her mother with his secretary. Though she was very young, this had a profound effect on her. Unfortunately, her father's behavior made her subconsciously believe that men could not be trusted, especially with the women they worked with.

This unresolved issue had followed her through all of her relationships. It was only after making this realization that Marian began to understand the nature of her jealousy. In a short period of time, she learned to talk about and deal with her feelings. Eventually, she was able to let go of her fears and trust the man she loves.

♡ *Allowing jealousy to run your life is a waste of the most precious thing you have, time. Talk with your partner and to yourself to ease this anxiety. If that still isn't enough, seek professional help. Life is too short to waste on this kind of pain when it can be replaced by love and trust. Here are some tips for keeping jealousy at bay.*

1. *If you have experienced infidelity in a past relationship or witnessed it in your family of origin, talk about it with your partner. Getting this on the table will not only reduce your anxiety and some of your jealous feelings, it will bring you closer to your partner.*

2. *Talk openly to your partner about anything they may do that makes you jealous and lovingly ask them to curb that behavior.*

3. *Give your partner some strong reassurance that they are your one and only. Even if there's no jealously at the moment, statements like this will keep it that way.*

Chapter
43

The Whole Truth

*W*hen issues come up in relationships, as they always do, some couples have difficulty expressing their feelings. When your emotions are in play, finding the right words or right way to say them can be daunting. Here are several methods to help you get started.

Many times, we hold back the whole truth from our partners, thinking we are protecting them, but we are actually trying to protect ourselves. On some level, your partner will sense you are holding something back. Learn to tell the whole truth from the start, and you'll save a lot of time and energy and be empowered to make up completely. It also will help to avoid continued misunderstanding. It's easier to have one long discussion than weeks of not talking and bruised hearts.

Making up needs to start somewhere. Even if you think your partner is to blame, you can be the one who begins the healing. Sometimes people really don't know what to say or how to start talking about mistakes they may have made. Reach out with an opening like, "Do you think this is something we should talk about?" This will speed up the recovery process and show your partner you're open to talking and willing to accept their apology.

Taking the first step is also a way of showing you care. Hold your partner's hands and look into their eyes when you discuss an issue. Looking someone in the eyes creates trust and says you are sincere. A touch of your hand can help ease their discomfort and let them know you are completely present for the conversation. This kind of connection is an important part of your relationship; use it as often as necessary to help create depth and tenderness.

Reading something relevant and passing it to your partner with the idea they will get it won't help resolve a disagreement. Sit down together and talk. Reading together is a means of getting started, but don't stop there; you have to actually talk about it.

Find out if you gave your mate what was required to resolve the issue. Ask your partner, "Did you get everything you needed to feel complete with this?" Share your feelings honestly. This will put the subject to rest and keep it from coming up repeatedly.

See if there is anything you can learn from your experience. Learning how to communicate better will prevent arguments and even a breakup. Once you both learn how to make up, arguments will become infrequent because you will seldom let things escalate.

These techniques will work, but only if you use them. Everyone makes mistakes; finding balanced ways to deal with them is a sign of a healthy, lasting relationship.

♡ *Here are some exercises to help you be wholly truthful.*

1. *If there is something you haven't told your partner, find the right time and place to open up and share it. I know this will feel scary, but if you keep holding it in, it will chip away at the foundation of your relationship.*

2. *The next time you have a discussion that requires you to say something that makes you feel insecure, begin by saying, "The whole truth is...." This will help remind you not to hold back.*

Ten Tips for Surviving Big Arguments

*E*ven the most caring couples can have a big argument that will cause hurt feelings for both people. Rather than going to your own corners to lick your wounds, here are some tips that will help you heal your pain and avoid having another round.

Using these tools will help you to return to your normal behavior sooner rather than later. Keep in mind that as long as you sustain the life raft of desire to reconnect with your partner, you can weather any storm.

1. *Know that all couples argue.*

It could be that you're tired or hungry, or that you're not feeling well. Perhaps you had a little too much to drink, or maybe the full moon makes you a little unstable. Whatever the reason, it happens because we're human and anger is a natural human condition. See chapter 48 on how to stop arguments before they start.

2. *Be patient. Remember that time heals all wounds.*

It can take a day or two to regenerate from a big hurt, so be extra careful with your partner, and don't disengage. Use this healing period to understand how each of you will behave better the next time.

3. *Don't leave.*

Hanging out in separate rooms to cool off for a while is fine. So is taking a walk around the block. But don't leave the house with a packed bag because this sends the message that you are leaving the relationship.

4. **Take 100 percent responsibility.**

    If both of you own the entire argument, your
    ability to fix what went wrong has doubled.
    Working together to heal a relationship rift is
    the quickest and easiest way to get back on
    the right path.

5. **Don't underestimate the power of apology.**

    If you hold fast to your righteousness, it may be
    all that you will have to hold in the end. Being
    big enough to step up to the plate and admit
    when you're wrong says a great deal about your
    character. People who can't say they're sorry will
    find it difficult to maintain successful long-term
    relationships. See chapter 41.

6. **Be kind.**

    Having an attitude after a quarrel is simply a
    covert way of continuing the conflict. Once
    you've decided to stop you should treat your
    partner with extra caring and consideration.

7. **Trust that you're loved.**

    "For better and for worse" are words to live
    by when things get stormy. Remembering why

you fell in love with your partner will reopen your heart.

8. Do something fun.

Go out for a lavish dinner, hit a movie, play with the kids or the animals. Being active with each other will create endorphins in your brain, which will make you feel better. See chapter 3.

9. Kiss and make up.

Making love after an argument is not an unpleasant way to reconnect, but sometimes it's awkward. If you agree to leave your troubles at the bedroom door, and turn each other on instead of the TV, make-up love will be unavoidable. See chapter 24.

10. Consider counseling.

If big arguments are the norm, or if there is more than 20 percent discord in your relationship, you should get some professional advice. Sometime couples get into a negative feedback loop, and a good therapist can help you break the negative cycle.

PART
8

Effective

Communication

Ask for What You Need

Have you ever been afraid to ask your partner for what you need? It's the anticipation of rejection that may keep you from asking. If you don't learn to ask, you will never get your needs met and you will remain feeling unfulfilled. Learning to ask for what you need is a big step in learning how to take care of yourself and your relationship.

To get your needs met, it helps to know exactly what you want. You can feel empty but not know what will fill you up. It's also important to believe you deserve to have your needs fulfilled. If you feel unworthy, your partner will respond accordingly. If you are in a relationship with someone, you deserve to state your needs and, if possible, have them met.

It is easier to ask for something when it is a real need rather than a desire. Distinguishing between a need and a desire is like distinguishing between hunger and appetite.

If your partner feels what you're asking for is selfish or not vital, they will find it easier to turn you down. You must truly believe that what you're asking for is important enough for your partner to stop what they are doing to tend to your needs. And be careful to stay in balance and be aware of your true motivation before confronting your partner with an issue.

Your fears about not getting your needs met may be so great that you may just decide not to ask. Sometimes it can seem like it takes too much time, effort, and energy. If you are used to having your needs not met, you may have decided it's no longer worth asking. Don't let the past keep you from getting what you need now. Just ask. You may be pleased to discover your partner is willing to be there for you.

Learning to ask for what you need is one of the basic rules for creating a successful relationship. It may feel awkward at first, but continue to discuss it and experiment with it. The joy of being in a positive, loving relationship in which both parties get what they need is one of the best things in life. Don't wait for it to come to you; ask for it.

♡   *Here are four tools to help you learn how to ask for what you need:*

1.   *To get the feeling of what it's like to be taken care of, practice asking your partner for little things. This will teach you that it is okay for you to ask.*

2.   *Ask your partner if this is a good time for the two of you to talk. Make sure they are fully there for you.*

3.   *If you get turned down, ask your partner how they would like to be approached when you need them. To compel your partner to be there for you, practice changing the way you ask.*

4.   *Encourage your partner to ask for what they need. As you meet these needs and the process becomes familiar, your partner will learn to respond to your needs in the same fashion.*

Chapter 46

Who Says Men Don't Talk?

I recently overheard two women chatting in the market. One asked the other, "Does your husband talk to you?" Her companion answered, "Of course he talks. He has to ask me what's for dinner, doesn't he?"

I understand where they were coming from. Most men have a hard time communicating anything that remotely resembles an emotion. Why? Because emotions are scary to men. Much of the time, many men don't even know what or how they are feeling.

It is interesting to note that women think and feel at the same time, while most men can only do one at a time. This difference developed back in the Stone Age when the man always had to be on the lookout for attack from some primitive beast, so being emotional could cost them their lives. The need to be a protector is hardwired into their DNA. Add to that most men's reluctance to embrace their feminine side, and it's no wonder they do their level best to stay in their heads.

Guys figure that once they have said the fateful words "I love you," and the relationship is in full swing, there are only three reasons to have a real conversation: sex, money, or breaking-up.

When a woman wants to talk, and the guy realizes he has to think and feel at the same time, just the idea becomes a challenge. So it's easy to understand why men have a harder time talking about feelings. It's because they have to switch gears from their head to their hearts. Sometimes when they have to do it quickly, they may feel like the life is being sucked out of them.

Most of the time, when a man wants to talk, he's thinking, "What do you want to do this weekend?" When a woman says, "let's talk," guys go to this place in their heads where they start to think, "Oh my God, what did I do now?" Many feel that their relationship is being threatened. What men need to understand is that when a woman says she wants to talk, she's saying, "I want to be closer."

There are some other interesting facts that can enlighten us as to why it seems that "men don't talk." For example, women have twice as many words as men. According to Gary Smalley, author of *Making Love Last Forever* (1996), in the course of a day a woman speaks 25,000 words whereas a man only uses 12,000. Perhaps one of the reasons why men don't feel comfortable talking is because most women can outspeak them.

Men and women also have different conversational styles. Women tend to talk faster when they get excited and may interrupt their partners who are struggling to find the right words. When this happens, their male counterparts may lose track or shut down because they feel cut off and unable to express what they're feeling. Men find it more difficult to attach words to emotions and getting back on track in an emotional conversation can be very difficult for them.

Understanding how men and women differ when it comes to talking will give everyone a little more empathy when it comes to discussing emotional issues. And understanding one another is a big step when it comes to creating and maintaining an emotionally fit relationship.

♡ *Here are some conversational tips.*

1. *Call your partner on the way home from work and continue the conversation once you get home. If you're interested in romance, this is a great way to start the verbal foreplay.*

2. *When your partner wants to talk, stop what you are doing and look into their eyes. This is a very powerful way to say to the one you love, "You are the most important thing in the world to me right now."*

3. *If you can't stop at that moment, make a date or an appointment to have the conversation later. This creates continuity and doesn't leave your partner hanging on to an unfinished thought or discussion.*

Share Your Feelings Daily

*E*very action or nonaction is a form of communication. Silence is sometimes the loudest form that communication can take. Without saying a word, you can easily express displeasure or anger. This expression through repression is unhealthy for relationships and for the person holding on to the feelings. It is so simple to ease tension with just a few words. It is anger and the need for control that allows you to hold on to these destructive emotions. It is much healthier to express your feelings every day, even if they're not positive. It cures the pain, allows you to grow emotionally, and strengthens your relationship.

Holding on to negative feelings can cause physical as well as emotional problems. Headaches, stomachaches, and insomnia are just a few of the physical symptoms of not discussing your feelings. As the feelings build, they become more difficult to express. This buildup of nonexpressed feelings decreases your tolerance level, and you may tend to lash out at your partner more often and with greater force. Most people cannot live in a relationship with this kind of anger for very long.

Many couples share this problem. Take Harry and Sally. Sally would be angry with Harry and would choose not to share the reasons why. She would act as if everything were fine and stuff her feelings. Inwardly, she was storming, but outwardly, she would pretend life was as calm as could be. Her partner would pick up on the unspoken feelings and subconsciously participate in the same game. When the pressure got to be too great, the two would explode and have a loud, hurtful argument. This would release the superficial pressure, but they would have the same argument over and over again. Accusations and blame were making the foundation of their relationship shaky.

The couple was feeling unbearable pain; splitting up seemed the only course of action left to them. The problem with ending the relationship was that they still loved each other. They needed a way out of this vicious cycle they had created. After some therapy, which included anger release and management work, they came to a place where they could agree to let go of the past. They made an agreement to never go to bed angry. When anger came up for them, they would talk about it. Most of the time, their issues had more to do with everyday struggles than with any difficulties they had with each other. They learned that they just needed to express their discontentment to someone who would hear them nonjudgmentally. They became comfortable doing that with each other.

When you can talk about things that upset you, you have become a real adult. With that also comes the ability to feel the joy of what a real and supportive partnership has to offer.

Being willing to take care of your relationship issues as soon as possible is a great gift that you can give to each other. It brings with it a freedom and a peace of mind that creates the space for the deepest kind of love. Knowing that there is tremendous joy waiting for you will make it easier to share your feelings on a daily basis.

♡ *When you're unable to talk about something that's bothering you, write it down. Think of it as a script to help you share your feelings and clear the air. Writing it down will assist you in verbalizing your feelings to your partner.*

Stop Arguments Before They Start

One of the most common complaints heard in therapy is that "My husband doesn't know how I'm feeling," or, "If my wife really loved me, she'd know how I feel."

Most people expect their partners to be able to read their minds. Few of us have psychics for significant others, however. Agonizing as it may be, we must learn to tell our partners how we are feeling.

Why does miscommunication create such a problem? Because unspoken feelings are picked up on an intuitive level. When our partners are angry with us, they can and often do communicate it without saying a word. The key to better communication and a better relationship is to learn to speak what you feel before it becomes a sore spot.

Trusting that your feelings need to be honored, not justified, is a crucial step in communication. It may seem like an impossible task. When you begin to take responsibility for your own feelings by appropriately sharing them with your partner, then each of you grows. Understanding this will make it much easier to communicate what's going on inside you. When sharing becomes second nature, you will no longer hold on to feelings that can damage your relationship.

By just choosing the correct words, you can invite resolution. The way you voice your frustrations may anger or hurt your partner. A great way to avoid this is to make simple "I statements" rather than cast blame. Statements such as "You make me feel guilty" are hurtful and just build more resentment.

Instead, take ownership of your feelings and try saying, for example, "I feel guilty about ..." or "I feel sad...." Such statements help to create a balanced conversation that will build harmony and trust. Often fights begin when one person feels accused and becomes defensive. Using "I statements" keeps the communication clear and prevents the blame game from taking root.

You accomplish two things when you communicate your feelings. First, you are taking responsibility for owning your own feelings, which means casting no blame and adding no fuel to the fire. Second, you are taking some action to change the energy. Both techniques open the door to constructive conversation and growth.

Here's an example of how poor communication can cause upset and how it can be avoided. Fred and Wilma had been planning to go to dinner and the theater for a week and Wilma was anxious to have a good time. When they got to the restaurant, the hostess seated them at a nice table. As they were about to order, Fred looked at Wilma, who was sulking. "What's the matter?" he asked in a concerned manner.

Wilma pouted for a moment and in her most disappointed voice said, "If you really loved me, you'd have known I wanted to sit at an outside table."

Now Fred felt blamed because he was unable to give her what she wanted, and the mood of the evening was lost. He thought to himself, "I can't ever seem to make this woman happy."

Both of them felt distressed because Fred was unable to read her mind and anticipate her feelings, even though being able to do so wasn't in his job description. Wilma needed to take responsibility for what she wanted and communicate to Fred her preference for outside seating. She also could have eliminated any blame by using an "I statement." Instead, she fabricated the feeling that he didn't care about her, put a damper on the evening, and may have created a harmful relationship issue.

The next time you want something or are upset with your partner, don't wait for them to guess what you are feeling or needing. Talk with them immediately, share your feelings and avoid blame by using "I statements." Communicating with your partner can stop an argument long before it starts.

♡ *Here are some tips to get you on the right track.*

1. *Sit down with your partner and talk about anything that's been bothering you about your partner or your relationship. Remember to use nonblaming language and "I statements."*

2. *Agree that if arguments start, you both take a five-minute cooling-off period and then take up where you left off. Keep talking until you both feel better about the situation.*

Honey, I Love You, But Ditch the Shoes

So, the love of your life just bought a new pair of shoes that in your opinion would look better if they were still part of the cow. You, as politely as possible, bring up the topic of Imelda Marcos or Carrie Bradshaw and their shoe collections as a means of broadening your partner's perspective. Now comes the part where either you bravely tell them what you really think or you mouse out and let them walk away believing they are on the cutting edge of foot couture.

Telling people you love that they may not look or be acting at their best is difficult. If they take it wrong, you could look critical or even mean. In truth, you wanted to save them from possible embarrassment. After all, they're the ones you love, and you want the best for them—if you could only find a way to say what you want to say without them taking it the wrong way.

Every loving couple will face this problem at some point in their lives. It could be your partner's shoes, their personal hygiene, or even their political beliefs. If you want your partner to be able to absorb what it is that you're trying to say without getting defensive, then you need to find ways to communicate that do not ignite their defense mechanisms. Here are some basic rules for offering advice. The statistics used below are drawn from a widely quoted study (Mehrabian 1971).

1. Whatever you have to say, say it with a caring tone. Tone represents 38 percent of communication, so by using a loving tone, your listener hears that you are really trying your best to help them be their best.

2. It's best to have the conversation face-to-face. Communication is 55 percent visual, and seeing the love in your eyes will help your partner hear you.

3. Choose your words wisely. Though words represent only 7 percent of what is communicated, using the right words at the right time can turn a criticism into a compliment. For example, instead of saying something like "The last time I saw shoes like that, the

Beatles were still together!", make a constructive suggestion, such as, "Honey, you'd look so great in those shoes we saw at the mall."

Couples in successful relationships know the techniques of sharing information, so when your partner makes a suggestion, let them know that you appreciate their opinion and insights. Doing so will allow both of you to feel good about yourselves and your relationship.

♡ *Here are some exercises to improve these kinds of communication.*

1. *Start and end with a compliment. Find something good to say about your partner. This will help them take in your advice and help them feel positive about the exchange.*

2. *Talk about the behavior, not the person. Feedback is not about insulting someone's behavior; it's about telling them how to be better.*

3. *Do your best to avoid hurting your loved one's feelings. Introduce the topic with a positive statement, and follow it with a gentle suggestion. For example, you could say, "I really love the way you talk to the kids. You would get a better response from your mother if you spoke to her the same way."*

Differences Make for Good Relationships

Couples survive religious and cultural differences, flourish amid backbiting in-laws, and even lovingly maintain peace while having opposite TV-viewing habits. Couples experience a variety of issues, ranging from feeling uncomfortable communicating their beliefs to arguing over whether or not to put a "My Kid Is Smart" bumper sticker on the car. Why is it that elections and political differences cause a surprising amount of disruption in some relationships? Politics and elections are polarizing. Perhaps because they're not about acceptance and compromise; they're about winner-takes-all.

Being at odds over politics or current events can make you feel anxious and fearful. It then becomes difficult for you to reach out to one another for your usual comfort and security. If one of you has a different opinion about how to deal with an issue, it can make the other person feel shaky. Not feeling safe with someone causes people to find ways to distance and shield themselves, and it brings up a lot of emotions. These feelings will come out one way or another, directly or indirectly, so they need to be talked about in order to avoid discord and discomfort.

You can do this in a variety of ways. For example, being able to joke about different political views is healthy. It helps couples understand each other and serves to strengthen your bond in an uplifting way. Some couples choose to share their views with heated debates, while others discuss their beliefs and fears quietly. As long as you talk with one another, even if you don't agree, your relationship will most likely not suffer. Communication is the key to unlocking any door that may appear in a relationship.

Couples without good communication skills may have arguments that can lead to destructive behaviors, like not talking at all or saying unkind things to each other. If this is occurring in your relationship, it is a danger sign, and you need to be proactive about finding and healing the real issues.

What's important here is that couples and families understand that it's okay to disagree. Differences make for good horse races and good partnerships. Being able to maintain a loving environment while having different opinions is the sign of a healthy relationship.

If you can't talk about your feelings, you will not be able to deal with the inevitable issues that couples face as they grow old together. It helps if couples continue to remind each other that agreeing to disagree is a positive part of a relationship.

Some couples make fun of their differences in a lighthearted manner, which is fine. However, if it ever gets annoying or hurtful, or if you feel that the differences are affecting your relationship, you need to seriously communicate about it.

Living with someone who respects you for who you are and how you believe makes life a little sweeter. If things turn sour, it's important to stop and find a way to give each other a little sugar.

♡ *Here are some exercises to help you create balance.*

1. *If your disagreement is so profound that you can't talk about politics, or anything else, for that matter, try writing your partner a letter telling them how you feel and what you need from them. Be careful not to send an angry letter. Releasing your anger in this way may be therapeutic for you, but it can cause harm to your relationship. You may need to rewrite the letter a couple of times to get to the heart of what you really need to say.*

2. *Another good technique is to engage in discussions with other family members about the current political climate. Talk about how it makes everyone feel, and let each person share their views without judgment. Having family members around you will make you feel supported and make it easier for you to share your beliefs and your opinions.*

3. *Talk about how you were brought up and how your parents dealt with their differences. You may find a connection with how the two of you are relating. Explore how your differences balance out your relationship. For example, if you're an introvert and your partner is an extrovert, it will help you experience more of the world and help your partner experience more intimacy.*

Change

$\mathcal{G}$etting the one you love to make changes can be fraught with pitfalls. Deciding on the best approach is really based on your partner's receptiveness and the depth of the difficulty. If the issue is serious, such as alcohol/drug addiction or abuse, it's best to approach your partner with as much outside support as you can get. If it's something less serious—you're unhappy because your partner watches too much TV—you can probably handle it on your own.

Remember to point out a few things that you love about your partner before asking for a change. Also, it helps to give your partner a reward for making behavioral changes.

If the behavior you want to change is minimal, I suggest using humor to point it out. For example, if you're uncomfortable with the way your partner dresses, try demonstrating how it looks to you by adjusting your clothes to mimic what you think they look like. Using humor will minimize the possibility of offending your loved one, and a visual picture can work wonders.

Sometimes art imitates life, and you may see your family dynamic on television. A little nudge to your partner, saying, "I hope you and I don't act like that," can open the door for a deeper discussion about needed changes.

If your loved one is in denial and does not see their bad behavior, you will need to validate your position by using good examples. You can also make a deal with your partner that it's okay to point it out when it happens again.

If you are coping with something more serious, I strongly urge you to do some research. These days someone somewhere has probably written a book or article on precisely the issue you are dealing with, so spend some time on the Internet and become more informed. Where your relationship or a loved one's health and well-being are concerned, you can't be too educated.

By the way, if you're going to ask the one you love to change, you have to be open to changing yourself. And the axiom of "Be careful what you ask for" is important to remember (for you may get it).

It has been said that the only constant in the universe is change. The problem is that when someone we love asks us to make changes, it can seem like a personal attack. If your partner does ask, I recommend that you view it as a gift, to help you be a better partner and a better person.

Truth be told, if not for the sometimes gentle nudges from my spouse, I wouldn't be half the man I am today.

♡ *If you want your loved one to make changes, the first thing you have to do is to get them to see the unacceptable behavior. This can be done in a variety of ways: by talking to your partner and pointing out what is disturbing you; bringing up the subject with the help of a family member who is also affected; or telling your partner how you feel in a therapist's office. Choose whichever method seems most appropriate. Then, go for it. Nothing will change unless you do.*

Ten Tips for Effective Emotional Communication

Communication is the most important thing in any relationship. Without it, you are doomed to a life of uncertainty and misunderstanding. Noncommunicative couples seldom last and usually end up living separate lives, which leads to separate marriages. Once you are able to really talk with each other, the blocks to risk taking, overcoming barriers, and letting go of ego diminish.

Here are ten ways to encourage effective emotional communication in your relationship. Even if you use only one of these tips, it will add to the depth of your communication and your relationship.

1. *Find the emotional connection with your partner.*

   Take a moment to look into their eyes, hold their hands, and reexperience the reason you fell in love. See chapter 8.

2. *Create an environment of openness; encourage your partner to talk with you.*

   Questions like, "What do you think was the best movie we ever saw?" are a great way to begin a conversation. Once the door is open, it's very easy to move to the next level.

3. *Make it safe to talk about emotions.*

   Let your partner know that you are there for them. It can be very empowering to say, "You can cry on my shoulder if you ever need to. I won't think you're weak. Your feelings are important to both of us." Once your partner knows that they will not be judged for being emotional and that their words will not be used against them, they will be more open to sharing their deeper feelings.

4. Help each other learn basic conflict-resolution skills.

Understand that in every conversation (no matter how heated) there is a speaker and a listener; when the speaker is talking, the listener needs to hear what they are saying. Then the roles reverse. This alone will make difficult conversations much easier. See chapter 44.

5. Encourage informality.

Learn to be relaxed with each other. If things get difficult and you feel like you're walking on eggshells, let your partner know that you feel the tension and that you are willing to lighten things up. If they agree, then kiss and move on.

6. Encourage your partner to bring their whole self to the relationship.

Let them know that they don't have to edit their feelings and that you are willing to hear whatever it is they need to say.

7. *Admit to your partner that not all of your actions, words, or ideas are good ones.*

   We all make mistakes, and we have to give each other room to be human.

8. *Encourage your partner to think out loud.*

   Nothing unsaid ever goes unnoticed. Even if you don't talk about what is on your mind, your behavior will reflect your true feelings. Talking about what you are feeling will prevent you from acting out and perhaps creating an unnecessary conflict.

9. *Promote the belief that laughter is good, and playing it cool is not.*

   A sense of humor may be one of the best things you can bring to a relationship. Couples who laugh together stay together and stay healthy. See chapter 3 for more details.

10. *Recognize that your emotional connection to your partner makes even the impossible seem possible.*

Having a strong emotional bond will help both of you deal with the inevitable difficulties that arise in life. Again, see chapter 8.

References and Recommended Readings

Barash, Susan Shapiro. 2004. *THE NEW WIFE: The Evolving Role of the American Wife*. Lenexa, KS: Nonetheless Press.

Beattie, Melody.1986. *Codependent No More*. Center City, MN: Hazelden.

Ellis, Albert. 1975. *A Guide to Rational Living*. Chatsworth, CA: Wilshire Book Company.

Glasser, William. 1989. *Reality Therapy*. New York: HarperCollins.

———. 2003. *Warning: Psychiatry Can Be Hazardous To Your Mental Health*. New York: HarperCollins.

Godek, Greg. 1999. *1001 Ways to be Romantic*. Naperville, IL: Casablanca Press.

Gottman, John, H. Markman, and J. Gonso. 1978. *A Couple's Guide to Communication*. Champaign, IL., Research Press.

Hallowell, Edward. 2004. *Dare to Forgive*. Deerfield Beach, FL: HCI.

Hendrix, Harville, and Helen LAKelly Hunt. 2004. *Receiving Love*. New York: Atria.

Kubler-Ross, Elizabeth. 1997. *On Death and Dying*. New York: Scribner.

McKay, Matthew, and Peter Rogers. 2000. *The Anger Control Workbook*. Oakland, CA: New Harbinger Publications.

Mehrabian, Albert. 1971. *Silent Messages*. Belmont, CA: Wadsworth.

Preston, John, and Julie Fast. 2004 *Loving Someone with Bi-Polar Disorder*. Oakland, CA: New Harbinger Publications.

Shea, Shawn. 2004. *Happiness Is*. Deerfield Beach, FL: HCI.

Sheffield, Anne. 2003. *Depression Fallout*. New York: HarperCollins.

Siegel, Bernie. 1999. *Prescriptions For Living*. New York: HarperCollins.

Silk-Forrest, Margot. 2003. *A Short Course in Kindness*. Cayucos, CA: L. M. Press.

Smalley, Gary. 1996. *Making Love Last Forever*. Dallas: Word Publishing.

Spring, Janis Abrahms. 1996. *After the Affair*. New York: HarperCollins.

Tannen, Deborah. 1991. *You Just Don't Understand*. New York: Ballantine Books

Viscott, David. 1974. *How to Live with Another Person*. New York: Arbor House.

Zukav, Gary, and Linda Francis. 2002. *The Heart of the Soul*. Old Tappan, NJ: Free Press.

Licensed marriage and family therapist, syndicated columnist, and radio host **Barton Goldsmith, Ph.D.**, is an internationally recognized counselor, author, and speaker. He has appeared on TV networks including ABC, CBS, NBC, UPN, and Fox and on numerous radio programs. He has been featured in national magazines including *Cosmopolitan*, *Working Mother* and *Bottom-Line Personal*. His weekly column, *Emotional Fitness*, which is syndicated by the Scripps-Howard News Service, appears in more than 125 newspapers. He hosts a weekly radio show on the most award-winning station in Southern California, NPR station KCLU, which broadcasts to Los Angeles, Ventura and Santa Barbara. In addition, he has written articles for more than 200 other publications.

Goldsmith works with couples, individuals, and families on issues ranging from addiction and infidelity to communication and abuse. He has trained with renowned psychiatrists Elizabeth Kubler-Ross and David Viscott. He is former professor of psychology at Ryokan College in Los Angeles, CA. The city of Los Angeles recognized Goldsmith for his work with survivors of the 1994 Northridge earthquake. He is a licensed psychotherapist and a certified addictions counselor.

Barton Goldsmith began working in the field of psychology when his career in professional basketball was cut short because he only grew to five feet six inches in height.

Partial List of Publications Featuring
Emotional Fitness by Barton Goldsmith, Ph.D.

Abilene Reporter-News—TX
Albuquerque Tribune—NM
Anderson Independent Mail—SC
Bakersfield Californian—CA
Birmingham Post-Herald—AL
Capital Times, Madison—WI
Chicago Sun-Times—IL
Cincinnati Courier—OH
Cincinnati Post—OH
Columbus Dispatch—OH
Commercial Appeal – TN
Corpus Christi Caller-Times
    —TX
Daily Breeze—Torrance, CA
Daily Camera—Boulder, CO
Daily Republic—CA
Delaware News Journal
Detroit News—MI
Detroiter Magazine—MI
Evansville Courier & Press—IN
Fresno Bee—CA
Globe and Mail—Canada
Grand Rapids Press—MI
Houston Journal—TX
King County Journal—Seattle,
    WA
Knoxville News-Sentinel—TN
Kokomo Tribune—IN
Louisville Journal—KY
Mobile Register—AL
Montana Standard—MT
Naples Daily News—FL
News & Observer—Raleigh, NC

Orange County Register—CA
Potomac Times—DC
Patriot Ledger—Quincy, MA
Pittsburgh Post-Gazette—PA
Post-Tribune—IN
Press Enterprise—CA
Press of Atlantic City—NJ
Reading Eagle—PA
Red Bluff Daily News—CA
Redding Record Searchlight
    —CA
Rocky Mountain News—CO
Sacramento Bee—CA
Salem News—MA
San Angelo Standard-Times—TX
San Diego Union-Tribune—CA
Sentinel & Enterprise, MA
SouthCoast Today—CA
Standard-Examiner—UT
Tennessean, Nashville—TN
The Gleaner—KY
The Stuart News—FL
The Sun—WA
The Sunlink—Denver, CO
The Tribune—FL
Times Record News—TX
Tri-City Herald—DC
Ventura County Star—CA
Vero Beach Press Journal—FL
Wichita Falls Times Record—TX
Working Mother Magazine—
    National
Youngstown Vindicator—OH